FOR THOSE WHO LOVE THE HILLS

PICTORIAL GUIDES TO THE LAKELAND FELLS

FOR THOSE WHO LOVE THE HILLS

Quotations from Wainwright's
Pictorial Guides to the Lakeland Fells

COMPILED BY

WILLIAM F. DYER

Additional illustrations by

REGINALD BASS

MICHAEL JOSEPH • LONDON

MICHAEL JOSEPH LTD

Published by the Penguin Group
27 Wrights Lane, London w8 5TZ
Viking Penguin Inc., 375 Hudson Street, New York, New York 10014, USA
Penguin Books Australia Ltd, Ringwood, Victoria, Australia
Penguin Books Canada Ltd, 10 Alcorn Avenue, Toronto, Ontario, Canada M4V 3B2
Penguin Books (NZ) Ltd, 182–190 Wairau Road, Auckland 10, New Zealand

Penguin Books Ltd, Registered Offices: Harmondsworth, Middlesex, England

First published in Great Britain 1994

Compilation copyright © William F. Dyer 1994
Text and illustrations from A. Wainwright's *Pictorial Guides*
copyright © Michael Joseph Ltd 1992
Cartoons copyright © Reginald Bass 1994

The material appearing in this book is based on works previously
published by the Westmorland Gazette, Kendal,

Filmset by Datix International Limited, Bungay, Suffolk
Printed in Great Britain by Clays Ltd, St Ives plc
Set in 9.5/11.5 pt Monophoto Bembo

A CIP catalogue record for this book is available from the British Library

ISBN 0 7181 4075 3

The moral right of the author has been asserted

The logo printed on the title page of this book
is a trademark of Michael Joseph Ltd.

This book is dedicated to
A Wainwright
who opened up the magnificence of Lakeland

CONTENTS

The fleeting hour of life of those who love the hills is quickly spent, but the hills are eternal. Always there will be the lonely ridge, the dancing beck, the silent forest; always there will be the exhilaration of the summits. These are for the seeking, and those who seek and find while there is yet time will be blessed both in mind and body.

PREFACE

In writing his seven Pictorial Guides to the Lakeland Fells. A. Wainwright became the constant companion of all those who have followed in his footsteps and tramped over that walkers' paradise. He was the greatest fellwalker of them all, which is rather a paradox as he invariably disobeyed the first rule – never walk on your own – and it is doubtful whether he ever told his wife or anyone else where he was going.

You have to read the seven guides to understand the immensity of the task he set himself and as a solo performance it must be unique. His refusal to accept help from anyone brought about the general impression of the man as a loner and his television appearances did nothing to dispel that picture. Thus many think of him as a taciturn, anti-social man who spurned any contact with his fellow creatures, particularly if they were of the female gender.

And yet in the guides there are passages of great beauty and more than a little humour. Surely the Introduction to the Guides, with which this book opens, must be one of the most evocative and loving descriptions of scenic beauty which has ever been penned.

For Those Who Love the Hills is compiled entirely from the guides and concentrates on the asides which are ever present in their pages, but which are too often overlooked. The extracts are presented exactly as written in the books except on a few occasions where additional words have been added in square brackets to assist in the explanation of the text. The Roman numeral in each reference gives the Pictorial Guide book number in which the relevant fell will be found, and it is hoped that readers will go on to enjoy more in the guide books because these extracts are only some of the pearls that can be found.

The passing years have seen changes which have a bearing on some of the remarks – for example, The Bishop of Barf's rear has been painted, and his friend The Clerk has been re-painted; Threlkeld has been by-passed, and bodies such as the Ordnance Survey, the National Trust and the Forestry Commission have all developed their policies and attitudes to meet the requirements of the modern environment.

It is hoped that this book will draw attention to the lyrical and humorous qualities of AW, as he has affectionately come to be known, though there must be some doubt as to whether he would have been pleased if it succeeds.

ACKNOWLEDGEMENTS

The quotation on the final page of text is taken, with her kind permission, from Betty Wainwright's foreword to *Memoirs of a Fellwanderer*.

I would like to thank my friends, the mountaineers of north Norfolk who introduced me to Lakeland, stood me on the top of England, and whose chatter produced the idea for this book; and to Jenny Dereham who introduced me so pleasantly, painlessly and professionally to the very strange world of publishing.

I

INTRODUCTION TO THE GUIDES

Surely there is no other place in this whole wonderful world quite like Lakeland ... no other so exquisitely lovely, no other so charming, no other that calls so insistently across a gulf of distance. All who truly love Lakeland are exiles when away from it.

Here, in small space, is the wonderland of childhood's dreams, lingering far beyond childhood through the span of a man's life: its enchantment grows with passing years and quiet eventide is enriched by the haunting sweetness of dear memories, memories that remain evergreen through the flight of time, that refresh and sustain in the darker days. How many, these memories ..... *the moment of wakening, and the sudden joyful realisation that this is to be another day of freedom on the hills ..... the dawn chorus of bird-song ..... the delicate lacework of birches against the sky ..... morning sun drawing aside the veils of mist; black-stockinged lambs, in springtime, amongst the daffodils ..... silver cascades dancing and leaping down bracken steeps ..... autumn colours ..... a red fox running over snow ..... the silence of lonely hills ..... storm and tempest in the high places, and the unexpected glimpses of valleys dappled in sunlight far beneath the swirling clouds ..... rain, and the intimate shelter of lichened walls ..... fierce winds on the heights and soft breezes that are no more than gentle caresses ..... a sheepdog watching its master ..... the snow and ice and freezing stillnesses of midwinter: a white world, rosy-pink as the sun goes down ..... the supreme moment when the top cairn comes into sight at last, only minutes away, after the long climb ..... the small ragged sheep that brave the blizzards ..... the symphonies of murmuring streams, unending, with never a discord .....*

curling smoke from the chimneys of the farm down below amongst the trees, where the day shall end . . . . . oil-lamps in flagged kitchens, huge fires in huge fireplaces, huge suppers . . . . . glittering moonlight on placid waters . . . . . stars above dark peaks . . . . . the tranquillity that comes before sleep, when thoughts are of the day that is gone and the day that is to come . . . . . All these memories, and so many more, breathing anew the rare quality and magical atmosphere of Lakeland . . . . . memories that belong to Lakeland, and could not belong in the same way to any other place . . . . . memories that enslave the mind forever.

Many are they who have fallen under the spell of Lakeland, and many are they who have been moved to tell of their affection, in story and verse and picture and song.

This book is one man's way of expressing his devotion to Lakeland's friendly hills. It was conceived, and is born, after many years of inarticulate worshipping at their shrines.

It is, in very truth, a love-letter.

2
ANIMALS AND BIRDS

The highest point, small and rocky, is a pleasant place for a halt and quiet contemplation of the scenery. Sheep think so, too, and wearers of new clothes should not sink into repose here without first clearing away the profuse evidences of their occupation.

(III *Calf Crag 6*)

The heaps of piled boulders on the fell, both on the south and east fronts, provide several safe borrans for foxes in their crevices, these refuges being well-known to followers of the Blencathra pack. When a fox is run to earth on Carrock the hunt is often called off and the frustrated pursuers retire brushless. Cheers for Carrock, therefore, on humane grounds also.

(V *Carrock Fell 3*)

Somewhere in the area covered by the map on the opposite page, *but not indicated*, is a small upright memorial stone roughly inscribed 'CHARMER 1911'. Charmer was a foxhound killed in a fall on Dow Crag, and it is rather nice to know that the memory of a faithful dog was revered in this way. But some visitors have seen nothing sacred in the stone and it has been uprooted and cast aside on occasion. For this reason it has been thought best not to disclose its exact location. Rest in peace, Charmer. They were happy days . . .

(IV *Coniston Old Man 6*)

Deep Dale and the eastern slopes of Great Dodd are abominably marshy. It seems an oversight of nature that the sheep here are not born with webbed feet.

(I *Great Dodd* 6)

The dogs of Seathwaite are friendly, and grand companions on the hills, but they must NOT be encouraged to join the party. They have work to do.

(VII *Great Gable* 15)

Until recently, the abandoned cottages in Wrengill Quarry offered a reasonably comfortable night's shelter, with bedding, an extensive choice of domestic utensils, and firewood in plenty. But now the roofs are almost gone, there are few furnishings left, and sheep have taken to dying in the living-rooms. For a bivouac, the open fell-side is preferable. And how the larks sing on Harter Fell at dawn on a summer day!

(II *Harter Fell* 7)

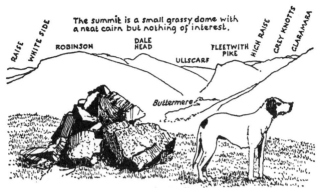

The summit is a small grassy dome with a neat cairn but nothing of interest.

RAISE
WHITE SIDE
ROBINSON
DALE HEAD
ULLSCARF
FLEETWITH PIKE
HIGH RAISE
GREY KNOTTS
CLARAMARA
Buttermere

The bystander, patiently waiting while details are noted but eager to be off, is Barmaid of the Melbreak foxhounds.

(VII *Hen Comb 4*)

The summit is a favourite haunt of birds, which have quick selective eyes for good vantage points. The Hobcarton ravens make a fine sight as they soar and spiral above the gullies and rock battlements, often alighting on the narrow top to survey the domain of which they are undisputed overlords; and particular mention must be made of the regular summer visitations of swifts, which have a liking for steep cliffs and airy summits, and here dart and swoop through the air in an ecstatic and erratic highspeed flight, their whirring wings creating a commotion of vibrating sound.

(VI *Hopegill Head 12*)

Nobody ever sung the praises of Trusmadoor, and it's time someone did. This lonely passage between the hills, an easy way for man and beast and beloved by wheeling buzzards and hawks, has a strange nostalgic charm. Its neat and regular proportions are remarkable – a natural 'railway cutting'! What a place for an ambush and a massacre!

(V *Knott 6*)

Many sheep-tracks cross the ridge from favourite pastures on both flanks.

Pause to reflect that these narrow trods are centuries-old highways for their users. They were here (and have not deviated an inch) long before walkers' paths appeared on the fells.

(v *Knott 9*)

By Lakeland standards (which demand at least a glimpse of rock in every scene) territory of this type is uninteresting, for all hereabouts is tough grass and heather except for the single shattered scree-rash of Brock Crag, above Fusedale; yet there is a haunting attractiveness about these far-flung rolling expanses. There is the appearance of desolation, but no place is desolate that harbours so much life: in addition to the inevitable sheep, hard fell ponies roam and graze at will, summer and winter alike, and the Martindale deer often cross the watershed; in springtime especially, the number and variety of birds is quite unusual for the fells. There is little to disturb these creatures. Man is not the enemy, only the fox and the buzzard. Loadpot Hill is a natural sanctuary for all wildlife.

(II *Loadpot Hill 2*)

(It is a contrasting commentary on a modern enlightened age that the most recent erections on the Moor are shooting-hides from which the harmless and helpless grouse may be killed and crippled.)

(II *Loadpot Hill 3*)

The neat little pass of Trusmadoor is the Piccadilly Circus of sheep in that locality, a busy thoroughfare in popular use when changing pastures, progression always being in parties, and in single file. The place is also well known to the

shepherds and their dogs, and to various species of mutton-eating birds that hover morbidly overhead, waiting for somebody to die.
(v *Meal Fell 3*)

Baby roe deer born to be free? or to be hunted and snared and shot by brave sportsmen?
(VI *Sale Fell 2*)

Seathwaite – one of the friendliest of farms. No need to fear the dogs or other animals here: visitors merely bore them.
(IV *Scafell Pike 15*)

There is heather on the eastern slopes, and therefore, inevitably, grouse; and therefore, inevitably, shooting butts: one may admire the construction of these butts while deploring their purpose.
(II *Sour Howes 1*)

3
ASCENTS

This wide scree slope, although not dangerous, is arduous to ascend, the feet often slipping down two steps for every step up – from which it should not be supposed that better progress will be made by going up backwards.

By the time the rowan tree is reached the feeling that one is pioneering a new ascent, treading where no man has trodden before, is very strong, and consequently it is mortifying to find the slender trunk of the tree elaborately carved with the initials of countless earlier visitors.

(VI *Barf* 6)

Sharp Edge is a rising crest of naked rock, of sensational and spectacular appearance, a breaking wave carved in stone. The sight of it at close quarters is sufficient to make a beholder about to tackle it forget all other worries, even a raging toothache. The crest itself is sharp enough for shaving (the former name was Razor Edge) and can be traversed only *à cheval* at some risk of damage to tender parts. But, as on Striding Edge, an easy track has been worn just below the rim on the north side: using this, rock-handling is kept to a minimum. There is one awkward place, calling for a shuffle off a sloping slab on to a knife-edge: countless posteriors have imparted a high polish to this spot.

(V *Blencathra* 25)

Some shelter here, and a rich soft carpet of sheep manure.

(VI *Catbells* 5)

This is the way the crowds go: the day trippers, the courting

couples, troops of earnest Boy Scouts, babies and grand-mothers, the lot. On this stony parade fancy handbags and painted toenails are as likely to be seen as rucksacks and boots.
(IV *Coniston Old Man 8*)

The terrace (identified by a little wall at the side of the gully) is wide and without difficulties but is no place for loitering, being subject to bombardments of stones by bloody fools, if any, on the summit above.
(IV *Crinkle Crags 17*)

The tortuous crawl up the 40 degree slope provides opportunity for observing the flora at very close range.
(VI *Grasmoor 6*)

Grasmoor is a very formidable object above Lanthwaite, its tiered crags seeming almost impregnable. The direct climb, up the angle between the north and west faces, is a continuously steep and rough scramble and a severe test in route selection.

On the whole, however, the climb is probably less difficult than the North Wall of the Eiger.
(VI *Grasmoor 6*)

Use must be made of a gap in the wall already occupied by a stream and the end of an iron bedstead.
(III *Great Crag 4*)

The Valley Route
This page alone is worth the price of the book to those readers who frequent Wasdale Head and yet do not know the Valley Route, for it will introduce them to a new way of reaching Sty Head, on a wonderfully-graded grass path infinitely to be preferred to the usual direct route rising across the stony slopes of Great Gable, and bring pleasure in future to what is now commonly regarded as a detestable journey.

There is as much difference between the Valley Route and the direct route as there is between sweet and sour.

It would be nice to keep the Valley Route a secret for the discerning few, and let the big parties continue to use the direct path (scar would be a better name for it), but as long as the present crazy urge for speedy methods persists (time is intended to be *spent*, not *saved*) there is little danger of the Valley Route becoming over-populated.
(IV *Great End 7*)

This route is an adaptation of a popular way to Scafell Pike (coinciding with the Langdale route thereto from Esk Hause onwards) and for anyone who sets forth for the Pike but finds his strength ebbing in the vicinity of Calf Cove it is a grand face-saver and will send him home with his tail wagging instead of between his legs, for nobody will regret a day that includes Great End in its itinerary: it is a magnificent mountain, scarcely inferior to the Pike, and, in some respects, to be preferred.
(IV *Great End 9*)

Although this is not the finest approach to Great End it is an

excellent walk nevertheless; but it should be undertaken out of
season if the idea is to get away from others of the species and
commune with nature.
(IV *Great End 10*)

But at 1500' Jekyll becomes a monstrous Hyde. Here the grass
ends and the scree begins. A track (Moses Trod) displays good
sense by escaping left to Beck Head at this point; ahead is a
shifting torrent of stones up which palsied limbs must be
forced. Only Moses Finger, 100 yards up, gives secure anchor-
age for clutching hands until a cairn is reached fifty swear-
words higher, where a more solid track (the South Traverse)
rises to the right below the rocks of White Napes to the
obvious scree-shoot of Little Hell Gate. Here, with the crags
of Great Napes forming a striking background, the horrors
recommence in even more virulent form.
(VII *Great Gable 20*)

From Wasdale Head this route is clearly seen to be the most
direct way to the summit. It is also the most strenuous. (Its
conquest is more wisely announced at supper *afterwards*, than
at breakfast, *in advance*).
(VII *Great Gable 20*)

Only those of unusual talent could go astray on this simple
walk, the line of fenceposts being a sure pointer to the top of
Brandreth.
(VII *Grey Knotts 10*)

The gangway is a safe route, but steep and sensational. Probably, more than 50% of those who try it will live to tell a
stirring tale of valour in high places. The casualties must
accept the fact that they were only ordinary after all.
(VII *High Crag 6*)

The unfrequented path on the north bank (right going up) is not as wet as the other – but this is not another way of saying it is dry!
(III *High Raise 6*)

This short climb is as simple as the diagram suggests, although not appreciably helped by paths. Anybody full of the joy of Spring will do it in 15 minutes (author's time: 35min.).
(III *High Rigg 3*)

A straight line is the shortest distance between two points. This route is the straightest and therefore the most direct ascent in Lakeland. It is also the steepest – a relentless and unremitting treadmill, a turf-clutching crawl, not a walk. There are only three opportunities of standing upright, three heaven-sent bits of horizontal, before the slope eases into the summit plateau. Looking backwards (between one's legs) there is a superb upside-down view of Wasdale Head. Back buttons cannot stand the strain, and wearers of braces are well advised to profit from a sad experience of the author on this climb and take a belt as reserve support.
(VII *Kirk Fell 4*)

The vast wall of Lingmell facing the dining-room of the Wastwater Hotel is unattractive, and it is asking a lot of a man who has eaten well at the breakfast-table to send him forth to

tackle its 2000' of unremitting steepness, but the ascent can be made tolerable by using a path above the wall to join the obvious west shoulder above Brackenclose, where fragrant mountain flowers and noble views temper the steepness.
(iv *Lingmell* 5)

The final tower is very steep, but within the capacity of valiant pedestrians. If, however, it looks too intimidating it can be avoided easily by grass ledges to the right – but this is cheating!
(v *Lonscale Fell* 5)

When fellwalking, it is better to arrive than to travel hopefully and this is justification for the inclusion here of six pages of directions for reaching the summit of Loughrigg Fell, because although of insignificant altitude, the fell has an extensive and confusing top, the ultimate objective remains hidden on the approach, and the maze of paths needs careful unravelling – besides, failure would be *too* humiliating!
(iii *Loughrigg Fell* 5)

Nonetheless, as a walk it [Jack's Rake] is both *difficult* and *awkward*: in fact, for much of the way the body is propelled forwards by a series of convulsions unrelated to normal walking, the knees and elbows contributing as much to progress as hands and feet. Walkers who can still put their toes in their mouths and bring their knees up to their chins may embark upon the ascent confidently; others, unable to perform these tests, will find the route arduous.

Care should be taken to avoid falling down the precipice or sending stones over the edge. Falling bodies, human or mineral, may constitute a danger to unseen climbers on the rocks or the scree below, or to grazing sheep.
(iii *Pavey Ark* 5)

. . . second (ascent): direct up the south scree, a continuously steep and unpleasant scramble in prickly, unstable scree; the route is dry and dusty . . . splintery stones and debris heaps litter this desperate climb. In a buttoned-up plastic mac, the ascent is purgatory.
(III *Pike o' Stickle* 5)

The direct climb up Middle Dodd is only for pedestrians suffering from a surplus of energy: they will get rid of it on this treadmill.
(I *Red Screes* 6)

It is possible to drop dead on this route but not to get lost.
(VI *Sail* 3)

This cleft is a tight squeeze, well named as 'Fat Man's Agony', and ladies too, whose statistics are too vital, will have an uncomfortable time in it. The platform is shut in by smooth walls, the route of exit (for experts only) being up the scratched corner on the left. But for mere pedestrians the platform is the limit of their exploration and they should return through the cleft, resolving, as is customary, to do the climb next time. The author first made this resolve in 1930 and has repeated it a score of times since then; his continuing disappointment is amply compensated by the pleasure of going on living.
(IV *Scafell* 3)

The first section [of Lord's Rake] calls for strenuous effort, as the assortment of buttons, boot soles, dentures, broken pipes and other domestic articles scattered *en route* testifies. The best footing higher up is at the right side. In a place like this, where boots cannot gain a purchase on the sliding stones and polished rocks, other methods of locomotion may usefully be adopted, especially when descending. It is no disgrace even for stalwart men to come down here on their bottoms, while ladies may certainly use their feminine equivalents without any feeling of shame.

(IV *Scafell 4*)

Many hearts have sunk into many boots as this scene unfolds. Here, on the shoulder of Ill Crag, the summit comes into sight, at last; not almost within reach as confidently expected by walkers who feel they have already done quite enough to deserve success, but still a rough half-mile distant, with two considerable descents (Ill Crag col and Broad Crag col) and much climbing yet to be faced before the goal is reached.

(IV *Scafell Pike 20*)

Waithwaite Bottom is dreary, and the gradual climb to the ridge lacks interest. For a diversion the author can only suggest a check on the number of his telegraph poles.

(III *Silver How 5*)

Both routes entail more hard labour than the tourist path from Keswick (which is easily joined from Applethwaite by taking the Gale Road) but have the advantage of being unfrequented and free from the two great despoilers of mountain solitude, litter and chatter.

(V *Skiddaw 14*)

Ask a Barkbeth sheep what the north-west ridge of Skiddaw is like and it will reply without hesitation 'C'est magnifique' (if it is French, which is unlikely) – which just shows how tastes differ, for most walkers, less easily satisfied, will consider it disappointing.
(v *Skiddaw 16*)

Very easy grass and very easy gradients give very easy progress. There is nothing of interest. Nobody is likely to drop dead with excitement on this simple, dull climb.
(v *Skiddaw Little Man 10*)

The Romans may have experienced exciting incidents when they pioneered their route to High Street via Scot Rake but twentieth-century walkers will find it a long, dull ascent, with little to engage attention apart from the tracing of the Rake, which belongs more to history books than to the maps of today.
(ii *Thornthwaite Crag 5*)

The approach by the lane behind the gasworks is NOT recommended, for reasons palpable to all who venture there.
(ii *Wansfell 5*)

From Dore Head, Stirrup Crag looks very formidable, and the upper band of rock unassailable, but getting up it is nothing more than a strenuous exercise in elementary gymnastics and unusual postures. The way lies within the confines of rocky cracks and chimneys, and there is no sense of danger or indecent exposure. Follow the trail of blood left by the author, or, if the elements have removed this evidence of his sufferings, the debris of dentures, boot soles, etc., left by other pilgrims, and step happily onto the pleasant top.
(vii *Yewbarrow 6*)

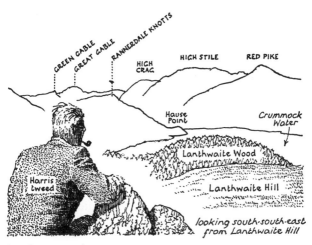

GREEN GABLE
GREAT GABLE
RANNERDALE KNOTTS
HIGH CRAG
HIGH STILE
RED PIKE
Hause Point
Crummock Water
Lanthwaite Wood
Lanthwaite Hill
Harris tweed

looking south-south-east from Lanthwaite Hill

(VI *Grasmoor* 15)

The author, after twice timorously attempting to climb the pitch with no real hope of succeeding, retired from Cust's Gully with a jeering conscience and went home to write, in capital letters, on page 11 of his Great End chapter: NO WAY FOR WALKERS.

Note that the wedged boulder itself supports a number of smaller stones which can only be at *temporary* rest. Heaven help anybody in Cust's Gully when they fall off. It won't be the author, anyway: *he's* not going again.

(IV *Great End* 11)

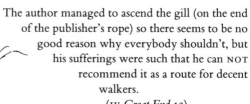

The author managed to ascend the gill (on the end of the publisher's rope) so there seems to be no good reason why everybody shouldn't, but his sufferings were such that he can NOT recommend it as a route for decent walkers.

(IV *Great End 12*)

Good stuff goes into little space, so it is often said (*rather to the consternation of the author, who is over six feet tall and fourteen stone in weight*).

(III *Harrison Stickle 6*)

There are fierce crags and rough screes and outcrops that will be grittier still when the author's ashes are scattered here.

(VII *Haystacks 10*)

The summit tarn

This is the view from the cairn on the summit ridge —
whether it coincides with the view from the highest point the
author will never know for his several attempts to mount to
the rocky pate of the Lion Couchant have all been defeated by
a lack of resolution; but probably it is the same. In any case,
most visitors will be content to study the prospect from the
comparative security of the cairn on the ridge. The Vale of
Grasmere is best displayed from the head of the other (official)
Lion, which even the author found a simple ascent (although
deeply conscious of precipices all around).

This corner [of the page in question] was reserved for an
announcement that the author had succeeded in surmounting
the highest point. Up to the time of going to press, however,
such an announcement cannot be made.
(III *Helm Crag 8*)

Buried Treasure on Lank Rigg

The only exciting experience in the lonely life of the Ordnance column occurred on a gloriously sunny day in April
1965, when it was a mute and astonished witness to an
unparalleled act of generosity. In an uncharacteristic mood
of magnanimity which he has since regretted, the author
decided on this summit to share his hard won royalties with
one of his faithful readers, and placed a two-shilling piece
under a flat stone: it awaits the first person to read this note
and act upon it. There is no cause to turn the whole top
over as though pigs have been at it — the stone is four feet
from the column. If the treasure cannot be found at this
distance it can be assumed that a fortunate pilgrim has already passed this way rejoicing. The finder may be sufficiently pleased to write in c/o the publishers and confirm
his claim by stating the year of the coin's issue. If nobody
does so before the end of 1966 the author will go back and

retrieve it for the purchase of fish and chips. It was a reckless thing to do, anyway.
(VII *Lank Rigg* 7)

The author carried out his explorations surreptitiously, and without permission (not caring to risk a refusal): he was not detected, but this may possibly have been due to his marked resemblance to an old stag, and other trespassers must not expect the same good fortune. Walkers in general should keep away.
(II *The Nab* 3)

The Abominable Snowman? No, only the author. (Not that there's much difference.)
(VI *Outerside* 1)

He will be a good man who can stand erect on the point of the needle.

   The author feels rather proud of this 'discovery' and hopes people will not write to claim (i) a knowledge of the pinnacle (since they were children, (ii) that they have climbed it (blindfolded), and (iii) stood for hours on its point (on their heads).
(IV *Pike o'Blisco* 8)

'First time we've seen him with a cap on.'
'He must be going bald or something.'
[Conversation between two sheep in an illustration]
(VII *Yewbarrow* 9)

5

DEDICATIONS

Book One is dedicated to THE MEN OF THE ORD-
NANCE SURVEY whose maps of Lakeland have given
me much pleasure both on the fells and by my fireside.

Book Two is dedicated to the memory of THE MEN
WHO BUILT THE STONE WALLS which have endured the storms of centuries and remain to this day as
monuments to enterprise, perseverance and hard work.

Book Three is dedicated to those eager explorers of the fells,
THE DOGS OF LAKELAND, willing workers and faithful friends, and an essential part of Lakeland life.

Book Four is dedicated to the hardiest of all fellwalkers, THE
SHEEP OF LAKELAND, the truest lovers of the mountains, their natural homes and providers of their food and
shelter.

Book Five is dedicated to those who travel alone, THE SOLITARY WANDERERS ON THE FELLS, who find contentment in the companionship of the mountains and of the creatures of the mountains.

Book Six is dedicated to those unlovely twins, MY RIGHT LEG and MY LEFT LEG, staunch supporters that have carried me about for over half a century, endured much without complaint and never once let me down.

Nevertheless, they are unsuitable subjects for illustration.

Book Seven is dedicated to ALL WHO HAVE HELPED ME – sometimes with advice, sometimes with information, sometimes with no more than a friendly nod or smile. They are too many to be named, and indeed some are unknown, anonymous fellow-walkers who pass the time of day and are gone. I must, however, thank my wife, for not standing in my way, and a few special friends who would not ask for identification here, for making the way easier for me to travel. It has been a long and lonely way, but I have trodden it increasingly aware of the goodwill and encouragement of many kind people, most of whom I shall never meet. And now, after thirteen years, I have come to the end of it and my final task, a difficult one, is to find words adequate to express my appreciation to everybody who has helped. The least I can do, and the most I can do, is to acknowledge my debt by this dedication.

6
DESCENTS

This is the sort of place that everybody would get down in a flash if a £5 note was waiting to be picked up on the scree below, but, without such an inducement, there is much wavering on the brink. Chicken-hearted walkers, muttering something about discretion being the better part of valour, will sneak away and circumvent the difficulty by following the author's footsteps around the left flank of the buttress forming the retaining wall of the gully, where grassy ledges enable the foot of the gully to be reached without trouble; here they may sit and watch, with ill-concealed grins, the discomfiture of other tourists who may come along.
(IV *Crinkle Crags 16*)

There must be no thought of a quick romp straight down to the valley immediately below: *it cannot be done*. Unless the route on the Stonethwaite face is already known, it should not be sought from above: the crags form an almost continuous barrier here. Paplitations and alarms may be avoided by following the wall down towards Greenup, and when rough ground appears ahead, making a wide detour to the right to join the Greenup path down easy bracken slopes. In bad

weather, or if there is deep snow, this is the only route that
will ensure the due arrival of the walker at Stonethwaite in
one unbroken piece.
(*III Eagle Crag 5*)

Too many cairns are worse than too few, and it is unfortunate
that the tops of the buttresses of the north face are unnecessarily
adorned with piles of stones, snares in mist for strangers to the
fell, who may think they indicate ways off the summit. So
they do – sudden ways off.
(*I Fairfield 9*)

Descents may be made in any direction after consulting the
map. No terrors will be met, even in mist; no discomfort will
be suffered except wet feet.
(*VII Gavel Fell 7*)

The only advice that can be
given to a novice lost on
Haystacks *in mist* is that
he should kneel down and
pray for safe deliverance.
(*VII Haystacks 10*)

If, however, Helm Crag is to be a part only of the day's
programme (e.g. the circuit of Far Easedale or the Greenburn valley) it is better reserved for descent, for then the
Vale of Grasmere will be directly in view ahead; and this
fair scene is at its best when the shadows of evening are

lengthening, with the Langdales silhouetted in rugged outline against the sunset. Tarry long over this exquisite picture of serenity and peace, and memorise it for the long winter of exile!

(III *Helm Crag 4*)

In mist, this initial section looks intimidating, but step bravely into the void and go cautiously. Anybody who finds himself falling through space will have missed the route.

(VI *Hopegill Head 12*)

Grass is reached at 2000′, and from this point onwards a badly-shod walker will suffer many slips and spills, none fatal, and it is not a bad plan to continue in bare or stockinged feet, which give a better grip than boots.

(VII *Kirk Fell 6*)

But the grassy slopes may be descended with ease anywhere – indeed, if nobody is watching, rapid progression by roly-poly may be indulged in by the young in heart; but *mind that swamp!*

(V *Longlands Fell 4*)

If returning to Buttermere, Ennerdale and the High Stile range will have to be crossed again towards the end of an exhausting day. There is no sadder sight than a Buttermere-bound pedestrian crossing Scarth Gap on his hands and knees as the shadows of the evening steal o'er the scene. The route is therefore recommended for strong walkers only.

(VII *Pillar 14*)

The best way down to Ambleside is by the south ridge – it is so easy a saunter that the hands need be taken from the pockets only once, to negotiate a stile.

(I *Red Screes 7*)

For details of the Rake, see page 4, where it is described in
ascent – it will occur to the mentally alert that if there are 3
ups and 2 downs in the ascent there must be 3 downs and 2
ups in the descent.
(IV *Scafell 14*)

These rocks are above the steep and rough Greenburn face.
Descents here should be eschewed. (Eschewed means don't do
it!)
(IV *Swirl How 9*)

7
FELLS

A unique feature that catches the eye from miles distant is the upstanding pinnacle long known as the Bishop of Barf, a venerable figure whose spotless vestments result from regular applications of whitewash by volunteers from the little community centred on the Swan Hotel directly below. This is a task not lightly to be undertaken, for the stiff climb to his pulpit up shifting scree is a bad enough scramble without the grave added responsibility of balancing a bucket that must not be spilled. But the job must be done from time to time: the Swan Hotel bereft of the benign presence of its old established and effective publicity agent is quite unthinkable. The two go together, even more so than love and marriage.

(VI *Barf 2*)

In comparison with the commanding figure of the Bishop, the Clerk is a poor drooping individual who attracts little attention to himself. He stands amidst bracken at the foot of the slope. Once he too wore white vestments (which are sadly in need of renewal, a few ragged traces only remaining).

A visit to the Bishop discloses that behind the spotless raiment he displays to the road below, his rear quarters are shamefully and indecently naked. Nor is he as tall as he may be imagined: seven feet on the shortest side. Nevertheless it is to his credit that he has maintained his stately presence, for all around is the debris of shattered and eroded slate; the Bishop is slate, too, although obviously cast in a sterner mould. The time will come, however, when a collapsing pulpit will topple him down the screes.

(VI *Barf 5*)

The attention of intrepid and well-insured explorers is drawn to the remarkable cleft vertically splitting the crag. It is not listed as a rock-climb, either because it is too easy or too impossible. It is certain to be dangerous. The author, still unnerved after his climb of Jack's Rake in 1957, has no information to impart.

(VII *Base Brown 3*)

This is the slope of Lord's Seat on which the 'seat' is supposed to be found, but its exact location is also in doubt. This doesn't matter either, the author having personally installed himself in every rock-recess hereabouts (anxious as always for the comfort of his readers) and found the process merely painful.

(VI *Broom Fell 8*)

Castle Crag conforms to no pattern. It is an obstruction in the throat of Borrowdale, confining passages therein to the width of a river and a road, hiding what lies beyond, defying cultivation. Its abrupt pyramid, richly wooded from base almost to summit but bare at the top, is a wild tangle of rough steep ground, a place of crags and scree and tumbled boulders, of quarry holes and spoil dumps, of confusion and disorder. But such is the artistry of nature, such is the mellowing influence of the passing years, that the scars of disarray and decay have been transformed in a romantic harmony, cloaked by a canopy of trees and a carpet of leaves. There are lovely copses of silver birch by the crystal-clear river, magnificent specimens of Scots pine higher up. Naked of trees, Castle Crag would be ugly; with them, it has a sylvan beauty unsurpassed, unique.

(VI *Castle Crag 2*)

Catbells is one of the great favourites, a family fell where
grandmothers and infants can climb the heights together, a
place beloved. Its popularity is well deserved: its shapely
topknot attracts the eye.
(VI *Catbells 2*)

Caw Fell, like many of us who lack a good shape and
attractive features, objects to having his picture taken and is
not at all co-operative as a subject for illustration. From no
point of view does the fell look like anything other than a
broadly-buttressed sprawling uncorseted graceless lump with
a vast flattened summit similarly devoid of a single distinguish-
ing landmark.
(VII *Caw Fell 1*)

Although cruelly scarred and mutilated by quarries the Old
Man has retained a dignified bearing, and still raises his proud
and venerable head to the sky. His tears are shed quietly, into
Low Water and Goats Water, two splendid tarns, whence, in
due course, and after further service to the community in the
matter of supplies of electricity and water, they ultimately
find their way into Coniston's lake, and there bathe his
ancient feet.
(IV *Coniston Old Man 4*)

A pleasanter prospect is the green strath of Gillerthwaite, but
even here, man, learning nothing from nature, has let loose his
fancy ideas of tree-planting and done his damnedest to ruin
the scene.
(VII *Crag Fell 6*)

Dodd, like Latrigg, can be described as a whelp of Skiddaw
crouched at the feet of his parent. But Dodd has latterly shown
nothing of the family characteristics and the old man must today

regard his offspring with surprise and growing doubt, and feel like denying his paternity and disowning the little wretch.
(v *Dodd 2*)

The fence straddling the top of Gavel Fell marks the parish boundary. Like the egg of the curate of the parish, it is of decidedly irregular quality.
(VII *Gavel Fell 6*)

There is nothing remarkable about Grey Crag, but here Lakeland may be said to start and moorland country to end – and the transition is sudden: the quiet beauty gives place to romantic beauty, placid scenery to exciting. One looks east, and the heart is soothed; west, and it is stirred.
(II *Grey Crag 2*)

Grike is undergoing a transformation. The Forestry Commission, denied further activity in the central areas of the district after making such a mess of Ennerdale, are acquiring more land along the western fringe, where they are less subject to public outcry, and Grike, like Murton Fell and Blake Fell, is now festooned with new fences and decorated with little trees that will grow into big ones, all looking exactly the same, trees without character. In twenty years another fox sanctuary will have been created, the landscape will have been drastically altered, and the pages of this guidebook dealing with Grike will be obsolete. Come to think of it, so will the author, God rest his soul.
(VII *Grike 2*)

No mountain profile in Lakeland arrests and excites the attention more than that of the Langdale Pikes and no mountain group better illustrates the dramatic appeal of a sudden rising of the vertical from the horizontal; the full height from valley

to summit is revealed at a glance in one simple abrupt upsurge to all travellers on the distant shore of Windermere and, more intimately, on the beautiful approach along Great Langdale. Nor is the appeal visual only: that steep ladder to heaven stirs the imagination, and even the emotions, and this is especially so whenever the lowering peaks come into view suddenly and unexpectedly. The difference in altitude between top and base is little more than 2000 feet, yet, because it occurs in a distance laterally of only three-quarters of a mile, it is enough to convey a remarkable impression of remoteness, of inaccessibility, to the craggy summits surmounting the rugged slopes.
(III *Harrison Stickle 2*)

The majesty and masculine strength of the Langdale front is itself quite enough to establish the fell as a firm favourite with all, even with those admirers who are content to stand on the road below and gape upwards, while for those who set forth to conquer, it provides a very worthy climb indeed.
(III *Harrison Stickle 3*)

For a man trying to get a persistent worry out of his mind, the top of Haystacks is a wonderful cure.
(VII *Haystacks 2*)

One can forget even a raging toothache on Haystacks.
(VII *Haystacks 10*)

Indeed, the whole fell, although of small extent, is unusually interesting; its very appearance is challenging; its sides are steep, rough and craggy; its top bristles; it *looks* irascible, like a shaggy terrier in a company of sleek foxhounds, for all around are loftier and smoother fells, circling the pleasant vale of Grasmere out of which Helm Crag rises so abruptly.
(III *Helm Crag 2*)

There is some quality about Helvellyn which endears it in the memory of most people who have stood on its breezy top; although it can be a grim place on a wild night, it is, as a rule, a very friendly giant. If it did not inspire affection would its devotees return to it so often?
(1 *Helvellyn* 2)

Gully-addicts will rejoice to learn that a long straight gully, full of shifting scree but with no difficulty other than steepness, falls from the ridge half a mile north of the summit, directly above the sheepfold in mid-Rydale beyond Erne Crag: this offers a scramble they (and they alone) will enjoy, but not even the most avid of them would find any pleasure in *descending* by this route.
(1 *Heron Pike* 3)

A high mountain ridge leaps like a rainbow from the woods and fields of Brackenthwaite and arcs through the sky for five miles to the east, where the descending curve comes down to the village of Braithwaite.
(VI *Hopegill Head* 2)

In summer sunlight there is a pleasant colour, the bilberry – greenest of greens – making a luxuriant velvety patchwork among the grey and silver rocks. In shadow, the scene is sombre and forbidding. The silence is interrupted only by the

croaking of the resident ravens and the occasional thud of a falling botanist. This is a place to look at and leave alone.
(VI *Hopegill Head 3*)

Ladyside Pike used to be known as Lady's Seat (a pleasanter name if interpreted as a place of rest, not as an anatomical reference), nicely matching Lord's Seat just across Whinlatter.
(VI *Hopegill Head 6*)

To walk all round it, having got there, is a rough tramp of ten miles. Meeting another human is outside the realms of possibility. Die here, unaccompanied, and your disappearance from society is likely to remain an unsolved mystery.
(VII *Lank Rigg 2*)

Latrigg is pastoral and parkland in character, not rough fell, and the summit is the easiest of promenades, so that this is not a climb calling for old clothes and heavy boots: 'Sunday best' is quite appropriate dress. New plantations and de-forestation have changed the appearance of the fell often during the past century, and not always for the better; at present the top is polled and thick fringes of trees at mid-height suggest an experimental coiffure by a mad barber. The woods harbour courting couples and other wild life and are not safe for solo explorers.
(V *Latrigg 2*)

Ling Fell is dome-shaped, like the top of a Christmas pudding. A Christmas pudding in its pristine state, has no ridges. Neither has Ling Fell.
(VI *Ling Fell 4*)

Standing Stones (only one remains standing – and that one leans badly).
(II *Loadpot Hill 10*)

Thornthwaite Forest
The forest should be avoided, especially the older parts, in
high winds, when the veterans creak and sway alarmingly,
and in gales, when dozens come toppling to earth – a circumstance in which the danger lies not in being knocked down
and squashed by a trunk but in being pinned to the ground by
a tangle of branches. Another *don't* is to wander off the roads,
into the forest, where ghastly privations in dense jungle can
be suffered before emerging (if at all) in rags. And *don't don't*
for heaven's sake start fires, or there'll be hell to pay.
(VI *Lord's Seat 4*)

A detour should certainly be made to Loughrigg Quarries, the
big upper cave being quite a surprise; there is shelter enough
here for the whole population of Ambleside (although, admit-
tedly, many people would be standing in water).
(III *Loughrigg Fell 7*)

To the traveller starting the long climb up to Kirkstone Pass
from Brothers Water the most striking object in a fine array
of mountain scenery is the steep pyramid ahead: it towers
high above the road like a gigantic upturned boat, its keel
touching the sky, its sides barnacled and hoary.
(I *Middle Dodd 1*)

To add to its other failings, Mungrisdale Common does not
lend itself to illustration. Most fells have at least one good
aspect, but the Common, from whatever side it is seen, has no
more pretension to elegance than a pudding that has been sat
on.
(V *Mungrisdale Common 1*)

This peak has great character, for shapeliness and a sturdy
strength combine well in its appearance, and that splendid

cairn etched against the sky is at once an invitation and a challenge – while the man has no blood in his veins who does not respond eagerly to its fine-sounding swash-buckling name, savouring so much of buccaneers and the Spanish Main.
(IV *Pike o'Blisco 2*)

It's a pity about the name, which derives from a Richard Robinson who purchased estates, including this unnamed fell, at Buttermere many centuries ago; thereafter it was known as 'Robinson's Fell'. But it could have been worse: this early land speculator might have been a Smith or a Jones or a Wainwright.
(VI *Robinson 2*)

A young rowan has secured a precarious roothold on this crag. Can it survive? Will some kind reader write to the author in 1970 and say it is still alive and well? . . . A useful bit of vandalism has lowered the height of the wall and made it easy to climb.
(VI *Robinson 8*)

Every walker who aspires to high places and looks up at the remote summit of St. Sunday Crag will experience an urge to go forth and climb up to it, for its challenge is very strong. Its rewards are equally generous, and altogether this is a noble fell. Saint Sunday must surely look down on his memorial with profound gratification.
(I *St. Sunday Crag 2*)

A man may stand on the lofty ridge of Mickledore, or in the green hollow beneath the precipice amongst the littered debris and boulders fallen from it, and witness the sublime architecture of buttresses and pinnacles soaring into the sky, silhouetted against racing clouds or, often, tormented by writhing mists, and, as in a great cathedral, lose all his conceit. It does a man good to realise his own insignificance in the general scheme of things, and that is his experience here.

(IV *Scafell 2*)

The western slope goes down uneventfully between Broad Crag and Great End to the Corridor Route, and the glory of the fell is its excessively steep and rough fall directly from the cairn eastwards into the wilderness of upper Eskdale: a chaotic and desolate scene set at a precipitous gradient, a frozen avalanche of crags and stones, much of it unexplored and uncharted, wild in the extreme, and offering a safe refuge for escaped convicts or an ideal depository for murdered corpses. Someday, when the regular paths become over-crowded, it may be feasible to track out an exciting and alternative route of ascent for scramblers here, but the author prefers to leave the job to someone with more energy and a lesser love of life.

(IV *Scafell Pike 10*)

Skiddaw and its outliers rise magnificently across the wide Vale of Keswick in a beautifully-symmetrical arrangement, as if posed for a family photograph. The old man himself is the central figure at the back of the group, with his five old children in a line before him (the favourite son, Little Man, being placed nearest) and the two younger children at the front. (Finicky readers who dispute this analogy because no mother to the brood is included in the picture (this is admitted, all the characters being masculine except sweet little Latrigg) are proferred the explanation that Skiddaw is a widower, the old lady having perished in the Ice Age – she couldn't stand the cold.)

(V *Skiddaw 4*)

Keswick people have an inborn affection for Skiddaw, and it is well earned. The mountain makes a great contribution to the scenic beauty of this most attractively-situated town, shelters it from northerly gales, supplies it with pure water, feeds its sheep, and provides a recreation ground for its visitors. Throughout the centuries, Skiddaw's beacon has warned of the town's troubles and alarms – 'the red glare on Skiddaw roused the burghers of Carlisle' – and today shares in its rejoicings.

Skiddaw's critics have passed on, or will soon pass on. Their span of life is short. Skiddaw has stood there in supreme majesty, the sole witness to the creation of Lakeland, for millions of years and will be there to the end of time, continuing to give service and pleasure to insignificant and unimportant mortals.

Let us at least be grateful.
(v *Skiddaw 6*)

Long may this charming, lonely and impressive sanctuary remain unspoilt (that is to say, undiscovered by and inaccessible to picnicking sightseers on wheels). Long may the road to Skiddaw House remain rough, gated and unsignposted, and long may the farmer of Dash be given strength to play merry hell with inquisitive motorists who venture on it.

The place should remain as a reward for the physical effort of reaching it on foot
(v *Skiddaw 20*)

The Little Man is so fine a mountain that it is less than justice that its name must forever acknowledge subservience to the parent Skiddaw. And 'Little' indeed! – the top soars half-a-mile above the valley. From the base of the steep and shattered western face three scree-covered buttresses rise out of the general angle of slope to appear as distinct peaks so far above that the walker here whose mind is saturated with Himalayan literature will irresistibly be reminded of Kangchenjunga.

From Carlesddam opposite, at 1700′, the whole face is displayed in truer perspective and the buttresses are seen to lose their identity below a single towering summit, the likeness now being more that of K2. (It is taken for granted that Himalayan enthusiasts are blessed with a little imagination.) The west face is quite tremendous.
(v *Skiddaw Little Man 2*)

The climbing of Steeple is a feat to announce
with pride in a letter to the old folks at home,
who can safely be relied upon to invest
the writer with undeserved heroism.
Fancy our Fred having climbed a steeple!
(VII *Steeple 2*)

The hidden recesses at the head of the
Kentmere Valley should be a place
of pilgrimage, at least once in a
lifetime, for Kendal folk, for here they
may witness the birth and infancy
of their river. But alas, Morecambe
is a greater attraction – and Hall Cove
remains lonely.
(II *Thornthwaite Crag 6*)

8
THOSE OF THE FEMALE GENDER

It is necessary in a few places to handle rocks but there is nothing to cause fear or panic, although ladies in ankle-length skirts may find odd places a little troublesome.
(VI *Eel Crag 8*)

(Ladies wearing skirts, in mixed parties, can best preserve their decorum at this point by insisting on going down first and rejecting offers of male assistance. Conversely, when *ascending* here, they must send the men up first.)
(IV *Glaramara 7*)

The route is almost sheep-free, and dogs may be taken. So may small children, who are natural scramblers, and well-behaved women – but nagging wives should be left to paddle their feet in Styhead Tarn. The journey demands and deserves concentration.
(VII *Great Gable 9*)

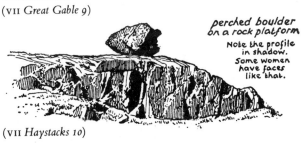

perched boulder on a rock platform
Note the profile in shadow. Some women have faces like that.

(VII *Haystacks 10*)

This section is really trying and progress is slow, laborious and just a little dangerous unless the feet are placed carefully; ladies wearing stiletto heels will be gravely inconvenienced

and indeed many a gentle pedestrian must have suffered nightmares in this dreadful place and looked with hopelessness at people striding along the smooth road on the opposite shore. The boulders end abruptly at a little copse of trees, and here, in between giving thanks for deliverance, the tremendous cliffs and gullies high above may be studied in comfort.
(IV *Illgill Head 3*)

Except for two short sections, the full length of the route is clearly in view from the Hause. *The wife, left in the car, will be watching every move!*
(VI *Robinson 6*)

One gate and the final hurdle, both of which have to be climbed, are surmounted with barbed wire and call for delicate and acrobatic manoeuvres. Long legs are needed to avoid mishaps. Ladies have shorter legs than men*, and should mind their bloomers**.

*This is hearsay. **Or whatever they call them nowadays. (A man whose only passion is for hills cannot be expected to be well-informed in such matters.)
(V *Skiddaw 19*)

It really is a matter for surprise that these fearful death-traps are not half-choked with the mingled remains of too-intrepid explorers, sheep, foxes, dogs, and women whose husbands have tired of them.
(IV *Wetherlam 8*)

9
HISTORY

There is a link with past days here in the names of the farmsteads [Iredale Place, Jenkinson Place, Hudson Place], which preserve the surnames of the early settlers and the original proud appendage of 'Place'. Most farm-names in Lakeland are either geographical or descriptive.
(VII *Burnbank Fell 2*)

A detour up the quarry road leads to a series of caverns, which for older walkers have a nostalgic interest: here in one of them Millican Dalton, a mountaineering adventurer and a familiar character in the district between the wars (died 1947, aged 80) furnished a home for his summer residence, using an adjacent cave at a higher level (the 'Attic') as sleeping quarters. *Note here his lettering cut in the rock at the entrance – 'Don't!! Waste words, jump to conclusions.'*
(VI *Castle Crag 3*)

The Antiquities of Stockdale Moor
In the uncultivated areas of the Lake District, many evidences remain of the former existences of primitive habitations and settlements, and these are usually found on open moorlands around the 900'–1200' contours at the upper fringe of the early forests, lying between the swampy valleys, as they would then be, and the inhospitable mountains. These evidences are very profuse in the area of Stockdale Moor and on the nearby slopes of Town Bank (Lank Rigg) and Seatallan.

Walkers should not visit the area, however, expecting to see a pageant of the past unfold before their eyes. Knowledge and imagination are necessary to recognise and understand the remains. A person both uninformed and unobservant may tramp across Stockdale Moor and notice nothing to distinguish his surroundings from those of any other boulder-strewn upland.

A name that arouses interest on the map of Stockdale Moor is Sampson's Bratfull, a concentration of stones dropped from the apron of a giant as he strode across the moor. So legend has it, but learned sources prefer the opinion that this is the site of a tumulus or barrow.

(VII *Caw Fell 7*)

Moses' Trod

In the years before the construction of the gravitation tramways to convey slate from Dubs and the upper Honister quarries, when man-handled sledges were the only means of negotiating the steep slopes to the road below, it was more convenient to transport supplies destined for South Cumberland and the port of Ravenglass by packhorse directly across the high fells to Wasdale, a practice followed until the primitive highway through Honister Pass was improved for wheeled traffic. This high-level route, cleverly planned to avoid steep gradients and rough places, can still be traced almost entirely although it has had no commercial use since 1850. Because of the past history and legend connected with it the early tourists in the district were well aware of its existence, and the path is kept in being today by discerning walkers who appreciate the easy contours, fast travel, glorious scenery and superb views.

Moses is a well-established figure in local tradition, which describes him as a Honister quarryman who, after his day's work, illegally made whisky from the bog-water on Fleetwith at his quarry hut, smuggling this potent produce to Wasdale with his pony-loads of slate. There is now no evidence of his family name, or even that he ever lived, but no reason either for doubting the existence of a man of whom so many legends still survive in the district.

Also attributed to Moses was a stone hut ('the Smugglers Retreat') hidden in the upper cliffs of Gable Crag, the highest site ever used for building in England. It is now completely in ruins.

Below this, in the lower part of the crag, is a rock-climb known as 'Smuggler's Chimney', not climbed by Moses but so named after its first ascent in 1909 out of deference to his memory.

(VII *Great Gable* 7–8)

Great Gable's summit is held in special respect by the older generation of fellwalkers, because here, set in the rocks that bear the top cairn, is the bronze War memorial tablet of the Fell and Rock Climbing Club, dedicated in 1924, and ever since the inspiring scene of an annual Remembrance Service in November. It is a fitting place to pay homage to men who once loved to walk on these hills and gave their lives defending the right of others to enjoy the same happy freedom, for the ultimate crest of Gable is truly characteristic of the best of mountain Lakeland: a rugged crown of rock and boulders and stones in chaotic profusion, a desert without life, a harsh and desolate peak thrust high in the sky above the profound depths all around.

(VII *Great Gable* 21)

One wonders what were the thoughts of the sentries as they kept watch over this lonely outpost amongst the mountains, nearly two thousand years ago? Did they admire the massive architecture of the Scafell group as they looked north, the curve of the valley from source to sea as their eyes turned west? Or did they feel themselves to be unwanted strangers in

a harsh and hostile land? Did their hearts ache for the sunshine of their native country, for their families, for their homes?
(IV *Hard Knott 2*)

The summit is barren of scenic interest, and only visitors of lively imagination will fully appreciate their surroundings. Any person so favoured may recline on the turf and witness, in his mind's eye, a varied pageant of history, for he has been preceded here, down the ages, by the ancient Britons who built their villages and forts in the valleys around; by the Roman cohorts marching between their garrisons at Ambleside and Brougham; by the Scots invaders who were repulsed on the Troutbeck slopes; by the shepherds, dalesmen and farmers who, centuries ago, made the summit their playground and feasting-place on the occasion of their annual meets; by racing horses (the summit is still named Racecourse Hill on the large-scale Ordnance Survey maps) . . . and let us not forget Dixon of immortal legend, whose great fall over the cliff while fox-hunting is an epic in enthusiasm.

Nowadays all is quiet here and only the rising larks disturb the stillness. A pleasant place, but – to those unfortunate folk with no imagination – so dull!
(II *High Street 10*)

The road to Scale Hill
The fame and glory have departed from the old road linking Hopebeck and the Whinlatter road at Blaze Bridge. Its rough surface is unsuitable for cars, and although the absence of traffic makes it a grand terrace for pedestrians, it is nowadays little used and, in fact, virtually abandoned.

Once upon a time this road was well known, and its sweeping view across the Vale of Lorton was a highlight of the then-famous Keswick-Buttermere round favoured by the early visitors to the district. This was the way of the wagonettes and the carriages in the days when a speed of three or four miles an hour was considered to be appropriate for a due appraisal of beautiful scenery. (Some of us still think so.) Eyes were more appreciative then and minds more receptive. Not one of the passengers along this highway would give a thought to nuclear bombs. Not one would be in a hurry. Those were the days of the artists and poets. The good days.

In these changed circumstances it gives an old-timer a certain nostalgic pleasure that the old signpost at the junction with the Whinlatter road still points to 'Scale Hill', a name that thrilled Victorian and Edwardian hearts but now means nothing to the neurotic Elizabethan lunatics who rattle past at 60 m.p.h. This old signpost is a last link with the days of sanity. But few choose to follow its direction.

(VI *Hopegill Head* 5)

The golden age of building passed away with technical advances in the industry, and the craftsmen died when the machines came. Once men built to last; now they build for the temporary requirements of a changing world.

Matty Benn's Bridge was built hundreds of years ago by men who worked with their hands and is still there, a joy to behold, and functional. But modern footbridges put across these western rivers too often perish with the storms.

The tragedy of our age is that we are not ashamed.

(VII *Lank Rigg* 3)

Rannerdale has a lasting place in history as the setting of a fierce battle in which the Norman invaders were ambushed and routed by the English in the years after the Conquest. Not even Gable has witnessed a real battle! And, what's more, our side won!!

(VI *Rannerdale Knotts* 1)

The packwoman's grave
Neglected and forgotten, yet within easy reach of the gill, is the grave of a woman who used to call at Langdale farms carrying a pack of articles for sale – and whose mortal remains were found and buried here 170 years ago. A simple cross of stones laid on the ground, pointing south east, indicates the grave; it has suffered little disturbance down the years, but because so many folk nowadays seem unable to leave things alone its precise location is not divulged here.
(IV *Rossett Pike* 4)

The Spectral Army of Soutra Fell
This is no legend.
   This is the solemn truth, as attested on oath before a magistrate by 26 sober and respected witnesses. These good people assembled on the evening before Midsummer Day 1745 at a place of vantage in the valley to the east to test incredulous reports that soldiers and horsemen had been seen marching across the top of Souter Fell (*Soutra* Fell was probably its name in those days). They saw them all right: an unbroken line of quickly-moving troops, horses and carriages extending over the full length of the top of Souter, continuously appearing at one end and vanishing at the other – and passing unhesitatingly over steep places that horses and carriages could not possibly negotiate, as the bewildered observers well knew. The procession went on until darkness concealed the marching army. Next morning the skyline was deserted, and a visit to the summit was made by a party of local worthies, fearful that the expected invasion from over the border had started (this was the year of the '45 Rebellion). There was not a trace of the previous night's visitors. Not a footprint, not a hoofmark, not a wheel rut in the grass. Nothing.
   There was no doubting the evidence of so many witnesses, and yet it was equally certain that the marching figures had

no substance. Scientists and students of the supernatural had no solution to offer. The only explanation ever given was that some kind of mirage had been seen, probably a vapourous reflection of Prince Charlie's rebels, who (it was discovered on enquiry) had that very evening been exercising on the west coast of Scotland . . . This beats radar!

(v *Souther Fell* 7)

10
INDUSTRY

Coppermines Valley

This hollow among the hills presents a surprising scene of squalid desolation, typical of the dreary outskirts of many coalmining towns, but utterly foreign to the Lake District, and it says much for the quality of the encircling mountains that they can triumph over the serious disfigurement of ugly spoil heaps and gaping wounds, and still look majestic. Here, in this strange amphitheatre, where flowers once grew, one sees the hopeless debris of the ruins of industries long abandoned, where flowers will never grow again, and, as always in the presence of death, is saddened – but a raising of the eyes discloses a surround of noble heights, and then the heart is uplifted too.

There is good fun and absorbing interest in locating all the tunnels and shafts of the old quarries and mines; *exploration must be carried no further than the entrances.* These workings, untouched for half a century or more, are in a state of decay and many are flooded. The shafts of the mines in particular, hideous potholes falling sheer into black depths, and without protecting fences, should be approached with great caution: we can't afford to lose any readers here, not with a further three volumes in this series still to be sold.

(IV *Coniston Old Man 11*)

mill.race

The Superior Sheepfolds of Skiddaw Forest

In these decadent years of easy money and overmuch leisure, of easy consciences and slipshod work, it is refreshing to come across craftsmanship of the highest standard and be reminded of the days when even the humblest servant took a pride in his work and when hands were the most skilled of all tools.

Such a man, a common hireling, built the circular drystone sheepfolds, six in number, that are a unique feature of Skiddaw Forest. (Elsewhere in the district rectangular shapes are favoured.) They are all within easy reach of Skiddaw House and within the forest fence. All are built to the same sturdy pattern, and although probably over a century old have hardly a stone out of place even today. These sheepfolds are *beautiful*, works of art.

The man who built them lived a hard life, working for a few pence a day, having to collect the stones he needed from the fellside and often sleeping rough on the job at nights. He did the task he was hired to do, and did it well. When, in due course, he passed away from this life he left no name behind him. Only his work remains. Just an unknown labourer . . . but how many of us today, with far greater opportunities and education, will be remembered by our work hundreds of years after we are gone? Few indeed! Idleness builds no monuments.

(v *Great Calva 3*)

Probably these were workings for the Glenridding lead mine, as is a cave in Glencoynedale Head, near the miners' path; here a warning notice – 'Danger. Keep Out' – relieves the duly grateful guide-book writer of the task of exploring its fearsome interior.

(1 *Hart Side 6*)

The Caldbeck Fell Mines

The older mines are now disused, most of them having been

worked from a very early date (sixteenth century or before) and been productive of a great variety of valuable minerals. The oldest and richest mine, Roughtongill, is reputed to have yielded 23 different ores and other minerals.

These places, for so long scenes of great activity, have today the sad desolation of death about them, but Nature is a great healer, given time, and traces of many former workings have disappeared except for the adits to the old levels. The tunnels and shafts penetrated to great distances and depths in the fellside, forming a labyrinth of subterranean passages along the mineral veins, and when it is remembered that they were hewn with primitive tools and wedges long before gunpowder was known, imagination cannot start to comprehend the skill and industry of the miners of those days, and one is left merely wondering why the fortunate workers of today are prepared to debase their vocations and professions for greater personal rewards. The Caldbeck miners had little schooling yet had nothing to learn about the dignity of labour or of loyalty in service.
(v *High Pike 3*)

Mining operations have left a few scars on Scope End, and some open shafts, levels and fractures that invite attention. Gold has been won here, giving Hindscarth its greatest distinction – but walkers who halt in their travels to search the spoilheaps for discarded nuggets will be wasting their time, the area having already been thoroughly combed by the author – also without success. Those who carry their search into the long-abandoned workings are unlikely to return.
(vi *Hindscarth 2*)

The lower eastern slopes of Raise are pock-marked with the scars of industry. The illustrations show the now-disused and derelict chimney and stone aqueduct which formerly served the Glenridding lead mine. Only a small portion of the aqueduct remains intact but it is sufficient to indicate the skill of the masons who built it and to make one envy their pride in the job, and be glad they are not here to see the ruins.

(I *Raise 3*)

Caves in Lakeland

Artificial man-made caves are plentiful, particularly in areas of copper and lead-mining operations, where tunnels, adits, levels and shafts are all to be found . . . Many of them are objects of great interest, and, if it is remembered that they were constructed manually long before the age of modern machines, of admiration too; but the strongest warning must be given to intending explorers that, except in a few cases, the mines and quarries have been unworked and abandoned for many years, and their subterranean passages are derelict, often blocked by roof-falls, often flooded, and supporting timbers may be rotted and ready to collapse at a whisper. In other words, these ugly black holes and pits are not merely dangerous, but damned dangerous. Sons should think of their mothers, and turn away. Husbands should think of their wives, after which gloomy contemplation many no doubt will march cheerfully into a possible doom.

(IV *Rosthwaite Fell 3*)

The square mile of territory between Tilberthwaite Gill and the Brathay is scenically one of the loveliest in Lakeland (in spite of the quarries) and surely one of the most interesting (because of the quarries). The valley-road is a favourite of visitors, but they generally have little knowledge of the many fascinating places concealed by the screen of trees. Here, in the quarries, it can be seen that Lakeland's beauty is not merely skin deep, that it goes down below the surface in veins of rich and colourful stone. Here, too, can be admired (indeed cannot but be admired) the ingenious devices and engineering feats of the old quarrymen of pre-machine days in their efforts to win from the craggy fellside this further precious bounty of an over-generous Nature.

(IV *Wetherlam 3*)

11
MAPS AND DIAGRAMS

The Mosedale appearing in the view above is not the Mosedale mentioned elsewhere in this book and situated at the foot of Carrock Fell. There are, in fact, six valleys of this name (signifying desolation, dreariness) in Lakeland and a pastime that might be adopted to fill in a few minutes while waiting for the rain to stop is to find them all on the 1″ Ordnance Survey map of the district (one of them is spelt Moasdale). If, having done this, it still looks like raining for ever, make a list of all the different names on the map in which 'thwaite' (a clearing) appears; this occupation will fill in the rest of the day until bedtime. On the 1″ Tourist Map there are 81 *different*, many of them recurring. Enthusiastic thwaite-spotters will find several others on larger-scale maps.
(v *Blencathra 31*)

It is a rare triumph to detect an obvious error on an Ordnance Survey map. On the 2½″ issue the 1500′ contour above Moor Moss is printed as 1800′.
(iii *Calf Crag 2*)

While the map was being drawn (on Saturday evening, October 4th, 1958) the last passenger train on the Coniston-Foxfield line was running its final journey prior to the withdrawal of the service.
(iv *Coniston Old Man 6*)

An error is admitted here. The tarn is named Styhead (one word, not two). Sorry!
(iv *Great End 4*)

But one cannot so wantonly ignore the authority of the guidebooks and maps; and the name Hartsop above How, without hyphens (in the belief that an error of omission is a less sin than an error of commission) will be used here in support of the Director General of Ordnance Survey.

(I *Hartsop above How* 1)

For the place-names on their maps, the Ordnance Survey rely on the information gathered over the years in their files, supplied or verified by church records, title deeds, estate books and other written sources, and often on the statements of local residents. On the Lakeland map, much reliance has been placed on spoken information volunteered locally (and in a few instances it would seem that dialect has not been interpreted quite correctly).

The Ordnance Survey map of the High Spy area is interesting because of the naming of sheepfolds. This occurs elsewhere in the district, but infrequently. All sheepfolds, of course, have identifying names known to farmers and shepherds, but not normally made public. It would appear, however, that the tenant of the grazing on Scawdel has been unusually communicative. Thus the Ordnance map names Joe Bank's (?Banks') Fold, Robin's Fold, and Wilson's Bield on 2½″ and 6″ editions, yet these are unremarkable structures bettered by many others elsewhere not distinguished by 'official' names.

(VI *High Spy* 4)

Note. The 1′ Ordnance Survey map shows the height of the depression as not less than 2100′ the 2½″ map as not more than 2050′. 2075′ has been adopted here on the principle of moderation in all things.

(II *Ill Bell* 10)

Introductions to each guide book

THE DRAWINGS . . . The drawings at least are honest attempts to reproduce what the eye sees: they illustrate features of interest and also serve the dual purpose of breaking up the text and balancing the layout of the pages, and of filling up awkward blank spaces, like this:

Don't waste time trying to sort out this untidyness [the author's own diagram]; instead, use the illustration given below.
(v *Knott 11*)

A rare and remarkable (and almost unbelievable) aberration on the part of a cartographer of the Ordnance Survey has resulted in Lingmell Beck being named CAWFELL BECK (in capitals, too!) on their $2\frac{1}{2}''$ map. One prefers to think that this is not an error but an alternative name; it is certainly inconsistent, however, with the $1''$ and $6''$ maps, which say *Lingmell Beck*.
(IV *Lingmell 3*)

A tree in the boggy wasteland of Mosedale is a feature worth noting, and the Ordnance Survey must have thought so too: they have indicated it by its symbol (◊) on both $2\frac{1}{2}''$ and $6''$ maps.

This is the only *single* tree in Lakeland so honoured. Oddly it is not a rowan nor a thorn, which might possibly have been

expected, but a holly, a healthy and flourishing holly, moreover, and a conspicuous landmark.
(VII*Mellbreak* 4)

For Patterdale and Hartsop, aim for The Knott to join the path there. For Mardale, use the ridge beyond Kidsty Pike – but the warning cannot be given too often until all old maps are out of circulation that Mardale Head is uninhabited, and the only beds in the valley are at the Haweswater Hotel on the *far* side of the lake.
(*II Rampsgill Head* 7)

Stones and boulders are not portrayed in this diagram. They number millions.
(*IV Rossett Pike* 3)

The compass symbol is aslant, but it's alright: it's meant to be.
(*IV Scafell Pike* 30)

12
MOTORISTS

The present road policy in the Lake District, of widening, cutting off corners, easing gradients and generally turning highways into racetracks, is surely wrong. Lakeland, once a sanctuary from noise and fast traffic, is being opened up to types of people who wantonly destroy peace and quietness and good order, and are aliens in a place of natural beauty. We should be putting up barriers to keep them out, not facilitating their entry. Lakeland is for the folk that live there and appreciate visitors who travel on foot or leisurely on wheels to enjoy the scenery, and the roads should be no better than are needed for local traffic. The fragrant lanes and narrow winding highways add greatly to the charm of the valleys; it is an offence against good taste to sacrifice their character to satisfy speeding motorists and roadside picnickers. Lakeland is unique: it cannot conform to national patterns and modern trends under the guise of improvement (mark the word!) without losing its very soul.

Let's leave it as we found it, as a haven of refuge and rest in a world going mad, as a precious museum piece.

Where are the men of vision in authority?

(v *Blencathra 8*)

No other summit of like altitude is reached so quickly and easily from a motor road. Indeed, if a car be used to the top of the pass, a man of conscience must feel he is cheating the mountain.

(vi *Dale Head 7*)

Car parking in the fields is politely discouraged by notices, rightly. There is peace and quietness here.
(VII *Gavel Fell 5*)

This is an excellent route for motorists, who may abandon their cars on the Pass with a height of 1190 feet already achieved, and experience the wind on the heath, brother, for the next five hours with no thought of gears and brakes and clutches and things, and feel all the better for exercising his limbs as nature intended.
(VII *Great Gable 17*)

Hallin Fell, beautifully situated overlooking a curve of Ullswater and commanding unrivalled views of the lovely secluded hinterland of Martindale, may be regarded as the motorists' fell, for the sandals and slippers and polished shoes of the numerous car-owners who park their properties on the crest of the road above the Howtown zig-zags on Sunday afternoons have smoothed to its summit a wide track that is seldom violated by the hobnails of fellwalkers. In choosing Hallin Fell as their weekend picnic-place and playground the Penrith and Carlisle motorists show commendable discrimination, for the rich rewards its summit offers are out of all proportion to the slight effort of ascent.
(II *Hallin Fell 1*)

Of course all rules and restrictions go by the board in the excitement of a fox-hunt. If the Melbreak pack of hounds rouses a fox in the plantations be sure the prohibited forest roads will be remarkably active with unauthorised wheeled traffic.
(VI *Lord's Seat 5*)

The Orthwaite road from High Side, although well-surfaced,

has not yet been 'discovered' (and spoiled) by pleasure motorists and is still very much a narrow country lane with high hedgerows frequented by roosting hens in the vicinity of the farmsteads. Rural England! – here is a bit of it left.

(v *Skiddaw 19*)

13
NOTICES AND SIGNS

Gain access to the paths through a gate that bears the inspiring notice 'TO THE FELL'.
(II *Angletarn Pikes 5*)

In faded letters, with Victorian courtesy, the old notice board requests VISITORS AND TOURISTS not to trespass in the deer forest.
(II *Angletarn Pikes 6*)

There may, or may not, be a signpost near the shelter. Signposts erected at this point never survive long, winter gales and campfires being the chief agents of destruction.
(IV *Esk Pike 3*)

Embleton Church is a mile from Embleton village and the bus route. Beware signposts in this part of the world that state the miles to Embleton, especially if there is a bus to catch – some give the distance to the church, others to the village.
(VI *Graystones 5*)

A signpost at Scawgill Bridge, inviting passers-by to use a footpath 'to Spout Force only' must tempt many people upstream in search of it. Only a few, grimly determined, will ever see it.

The signpost, due to the effluxion of time and in particular to the habit of young spruce to add a foot a year to their height, has become a bad joke. Originally it was provided by the Forestry Commission as a concession to the public, the waterfall in its rocky gorge being well worth seeing. Notwithstanding their signpost, the Commission then proceeded to plant the route with prickly young trees, which, with the passing years, have encroached upon the path and obliterated it.

There are evidences of violent struggle, man versus vegetation, and signs that some hardy individuals have forced a way into the jungle, emerging on an extremely dangerous slope above the gorge, but the nearest approach is gained by following the stream strictly almost to the portals of the gorge, where a water-barrier stops further progress. In neither case does one get a glimpse of the waterfall. A few yards above the stream, after more painful gymnastics, a forlorn notice-board is found in the forest and this announces the end of the path (joke no. 2). At this point an abnormally tall person could just see the upper part of the fall up to 1963, but from 1964 onwards the growing trees will have concealed it completely.
(VI *Graystones 8*)

This small stone tablet, 40 yards S of the shelter, commemorates the landing of an aeroplane in 1926. (Playful pedestrians may have hidden it with stones.)
(I *Helvellyn 21*)

A signpost will probably be seen at Greenup Edge. Less
certain is that it will have direction-arms.
(III *High Raise 6*)

If the signpost at Skelwith still says it is five miles to Grasmere,
don't believe it. Three is nearer the truth.
(III *Loughrigg Fell 10*)

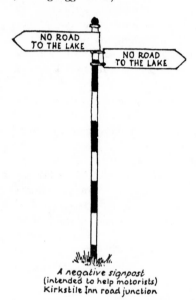

A negative signpost
(intended to help motorists)
Kirkstile Inn road junction

(VII *Mellbreak 4*)

Sixty yards south-west is a spectral signpost that once directed
visitors to Mardale and Patterdale but lost its arms long ago: in
any case its usefulness would be largely past, for few now
go to Mardale.
(II *Rampsgill Head 7*)

The monument is a memorial to three men of the Hawell family, shepherds of Lonscale. It is inscribed with this epitaph:

> Great Shepherd of Thy heavenly flock
> These men have left our hill
> Their feet were on the living rock
> Oh guide and bless them still

Simple, sincere and moving words that will appeal to all lovers of the fells.
(v *Skiddaw 11*)

Heaven preserve us from any more Public Boards but if there must be another let it be a Mousthwaite Drainage Board charged with the immediate task of irrigating the filthy quagmire through which the path starts.
(v *Southern Fell 6*)

A unique, ingenious signpost (of wood)

To ESKDALE

— artist unknown; probably the work of a forest employee. Congratulations on a bright and original idea!

(IV *Whin Rigg 6*)

In summertime the cairn often becomes over-run with tourists, and a seeker after solitary contemplation may then be recommended to go across to the south peak, where, after enjoying the splendid view of Eskdale, he can observe the visitors to the summit from this distance. He may find himself wondering what impulse had driven these good folk to leave the comforts of the valley and make the weary ascent to this inhospitable place.

Why *does* a man climb mountains? Why has he forced his tired and sweating body up here when he might instead have been sitting at his ease in a deckchair at the seaside, looking at girls in bikinis, or fast asleep, or sucking ice-cream, according to his fancy. On the face of it the thing doesn't make sense.

Yet more and more people are turning to the hills; they find something in these wild places that can be found nowhere else. It may be solace for some, satisfaction for others: the joy of exercising muscles that modern ways of living have cramped, perhaps; or a balm for jangled nerves in the solitude and silence of the peaks; or escape from the clamour and tumult of everyday existence. It may have something to do with a man's subconscious search for beauty, growing keener as so much in the world grows uglier. It may be a need to readjust his sights, to get out of his own narrow groove and climb above it to see wider horizons and truer perspectives. In a few cases, it may even be a curiosity inspired by A. Wainwright's Pictorial Guides. Or it may be, and for most walkers it *will* be, quite simply, a deep love of the hills, a love that has grown over the years, whatever motive first took them there: a feeling that these hills are friends, tried and trusted friends, always there when needed.

It is a question every man must answer for himself.
(IV *Scafell Pike 24*)

15
SUMMITS AND SUMMIT-CAIRNS

The highest point is a small outcrop with the ambitious name of Black Crag, and is given further distinction by the erection thereon of a triangulation column of the standard pattern to which has been affixed the extra adornment of the familiar metal symbol of the National Trust (this has been defaced by the scratched initials of visitors of the type who seem to see in this practice a chance of immortality. It must be readily conceded that, for people of such mentality, probably it is their only chance.

(IV *Black Fell 3*)

But a great humiliation has recently befallen it. It stands no less proudly, but man has seen fit to place a shackle around it, a shackle in the shape of a new unclimbable wire mesh fence, denying to sheep their inherited right to graze the sweet grasses amongst the stones, and denying to fellwalkers their inherited right to visit the cairn. The fence marks the boundaries of the land newly acquired by the Forestry Commission, but was it really necessary to indicate ownership with such precision? Nobody is likely to question the title deeds, and surely it is not intended to plant trees right over the summit, 1800 feet up and fully exposed to western gales? Could not the highest parts of the fell have been left with free access? If not, if possession must be demonstrated so visibly on the ground, could not the fence have been provided with simple stepstiles – two are needed, one to link with Carling Knott, the other with Gavel Fell. Dammit, if a man wants to climb a hill, any hill, he should be allowed to do so without being forced to commit a trespass. Why make the innocent feel guilty?

(VII *Blake Fell 7*)

This useful refuge is situated at the base of the prominent rocky tor 150 yards west of the summit-cairn. It cannot be seen from the path. The accommodation is strictly limited.

(III *Blea Rigg 12*)

The rugged summit provides poor picking for the Bowfell sheep, who draw the line at mosses and lichens and look elsewhere for their mountain greenery, and reserves its best rewards for the walkers who climb the natural rocky stairway to its upper limit, for here, spread before them for their delectation, is a more glorious panorama, which, moreover, may be surveyed and appreciated from positions of repose on the comfortable flat seats of stone (comfortable in the sense that everybody arriving here says how nice it is to sit down) with which the summit is liberally equipped.

(IV *Bowfell 11*)

Two fences joining on the summit [Owsen Fell] are unusual, being ornamental, not stock-turning, and erected on a dwarf stone wall. But high winds are no respecters of the elegant and the whole is in disrepair.

(VII *Burnbank Fell 4*)

There may be a cairn on the summit, or there may not ...
Sometimes there is, sometimes there isn't ... The frequent
visitor gains the impression that a feud rages here between
cairn-builders and cairn-destroyers, with the contestants evenly
matched, so that one week there will be a cairn, the next
week not, and so on.

(IV *Coniston Old Man 13*)

There are hundreds of unnecessary cairns on the fells, and
no great loss would be suffered if they were scattered, but
those on the summits of the mountains have a special signifi-
cance: they are old friends and should be left inviolate in their
lonely stations to greet their visitors. This was how it used to
be, and they were treated with respect. Fellwalkers knew them
well.

But not now. Lunatics are loose on the hills; not many, just
a few idiots whose limit of bravery is to destroy what others
have created. The fine columns on Pike o'Blisco and Lingmell
have both been wrecked in recent years (and rebuilt by
walkers who felt bereaved by their absence, and to whom
thanks are due). Dale Head's original cairn has fallen to the
destroyers, too: but here has arisen an even nobler edifice. An
expert working party has been on the job, and the stones
appear to have come from Yew Crag quarry. This new cairn
is unusual in shape, being wider at mid-height than at the
base, but it is a very solid and sound effort. Long may it reign
over Dale Head.

(VI *Dale Head 9*)

This beautifully-built 8' column, commanding a view of
Scandale, is one of the finest specimens on these hills. It is
more than a cairn. It is a work of art and a lasting memorial
to its builder.

(I *Dove Crag 9*)

Count this amongst the most delectable and exhilarating of Lakeland summits, for the sublime architecture of the great crag directly below is manifest in the topmost rocks also, forming an airy perch on a fang of naked stone elevated high above the tremendous precipice: a scene that cannot fail to exalt the minds of those who have lifted their bodies to it.
(IV *Dow Crag 10*)

It is obvious that this cairn is the result of much labour (for loose stones are at a premium on the all-grassy top) by an ardent member of the ancient company of Cairnbuilders Anonymous.
(VII *Gavel Fell 7*)

Gable, tough and strong all through its height, has here made a final gesture by providing an outcrop of rock even in its last inches, so that one must climb to touch the cairn (which, being hallowed as a shrine by fellwalkers everywhere, let no man tear asunder lest a thousand curses accompany his guilty flight!). On three sides the slopes fall away immediately, but to the north there extends a small plateau, with a little vegetation, before the summit collapses in the sheer plunge of Gable Crag.
(VII *Great Gable 21*)

The top is a carpet of excellent turf which many a cricket-ground would welcome.
(I *Great Rigg 5*)

It is a disappointment to have no cairn to recline against; and as there is no natural seat anywhere on the top visitors inevitably drift into the nearby wall-shelter and there rest ankle-deep in debris of countless packed lunches. The summit is covered in shale and is lacking in natural features, a deficiency which man has attempted to remedy by erecting thereon, as well as the shelter, a triangulation column and two monuments. And until many walkers learn better manners there is a crying need for an incinerator also, to dispose of the decaying heaps of litter they leave behind to greet those who follow.

(i *Helvellyn 19*)

But, up to the end of 1960, the biggest surprise of all was a wrought-iron garden seat, a contraption of elaborate embellishments into the voluptuous curves of which tired limbs surrendered gratefully: no other fell-top provided such luxurious comfort. Its very ornamentation proved its undoing, however, and it was removed and replaced late in 1960 by another seat – a structure of slate slabs, severely simple in design – after sheep had been found held captive by it, their horns entangled in the ironwork. Both seats, old and new, were placed there as memorials to Mick Lewis, a youth of Nether Row, 'who loved all these fells'. Which is a nice thing to say of anybody.

(v *High Pike 12*)

The top has pretensions to beauty only when the heather is in bloom; for most of the year it is a dreary place, with no

feature of interest. A big cairn offers a seat to travellers who wish to pour the water out of their boots. Nearby, in the old fence, there is a stile, now used by short-sighted hikers only.
(III *High Tove 2*)

If the party consists of more than one person, and if, further, a bat, ball and wickets can be found in the depth of somebody's rucksack, a cricket match can be played on turf that many a county ground might covet. Apart from this, no suggestions can be made for whiling away the time (unless the party be a mixed one), the smooth top being completely without anything worth investigating. The solitary walker, unable to indulge in communal games or pastimes, will find himself wondering who carried up the stones to make the cairn, and whence they came: must have been another lonely soul with nobody to play with!
(v *Knott 10*)

Although the top of Latrigg is a green sward it is pitted with the decayed stumps of trees long since felled, and a few solitary straining posts survive to tell us of the time when this popular walk was contained by a fence ... A thin line of untidy and unhappy trees has been preserved nearby – why? They are no ornament to the fell and from the streets of Keswick simply give the impression of a badly-shaven chin – or, more appropriately, the last few feeble sprouts on a bald head.

This is a grand place, all the same, especially for fellwalkers on the retired list: here they can recline for hours, recalling joyful days when they had energy enough to climb to the tops of all the mountains in view. Strange how all the best days of memory are to do with summit-cairns. . . . Will there be mountains like these in heaven . . . or is *this* heaven, before death, and will there never again be hills to climb? Is Latrigg the last of all? But no, it needn't be – there's still Orrest Head, even easier.

(v *Latrigg 8*)

Its furnishings of fragrant vegetation – small soft carpets of dry mosses, bilberry and short heather; its quietness, airy elevation and glorious views make this one of the choicest of summits. It is a place fashioned by heaven for the repose and recuperation of tired limbs – or designed by the devil for the abandonment of all further effort. Before composing oneself to slumber, however, it is well to reflect that the edge of a profound abyss is only a short roll distant.

(v *Long Side 6*)

Stones galore, all in a great heap on a felltop predominantly of soft turf, is an unnatural phenomenon that greets all visitors to Seatallan's summit. Cairns are not a fashion introduced by walkers. Shepherds built cairns as landmarks for their own guidance in bad weather long before people climbed hills for pleasure. And long before the shepherds the first primitive

dwellers in the district built cairns in and around their settlements and over their burial places. The big cairn on Seatallan
is attributed to the early British inhabitants and may well be
thousands of years old.
(VII *Seatallan* 7)

A feature of the ridge is a series of roughly-erected wind
shelters of stones, crescent-shaped to make them snug (they
fail lamentably in this object) – these are only partially effective against cruel gales and useless as a protection in rain. The
summit is completely exposed to the north and its weather
can be fierce.

Skiddaw is often described as 'merely a grassy hill'. But its
summit is the summit of a mountain.
(V *Skiddaw* 22)

The official altitude of Slight Side is a tribute to the meticulous care of the Ordnance Survey. But if Nelson had been in charge of the surveying party, and been a mountaineer too, surely he would have recorded 2500!
(IV *Slight Side*[*2499 ft*] 1)

When fixing the county boundaries between Cumberland and Westmorland the surveyors decided that the demarcation should make a sharp angle on the top – which is probably the most exciting thing that ever happened to Thunacar Knott.
(III *Thunacar Knott* 1)

A few big stones adorn the highest point, at the western end of the flat triangular top, and they look strangely alien in the universal grassiness of the surroundings, as though they had been carried there. (Maybe Mr Watson undertook this task: if so, it is fitting that the fell should bear his name!)
(I *Watson's Dodd* 4)

Peter House, Mirkholme and Dash are farms. In fact, the scene in the valley of Dash Beck is truly rural. There are no hotels, no private residences, no mansions. All is quiet in this lovely fold of the hills. It seems remote from the busy world, and much more to be preferred. Sheep and cattle graze undisturbed in pastures that tell of good husbandry over the centuries. Sometimes a solitary farmworker can be seen tilling the few ploughed fields, or repairing a wall, or 'doing the rounds' with his dog. Surely this is life as it was meant to be lived, close to the good earth? One regret . . . gone from the farms are the fine horses, not the less noble for being servants. Tractors and machines have taken their place. This, we are told, is a sign of the march of progress . . . but nobody ever tells us *where* it is marching. It's time we found out. We might be losing more than we are gaining.

(v *Bakestall 3*)

The Vale of Lorton is one of the pleasantest of Lakeland's valleys. Quiet and serene, it has suffered little by modern developments. In comparison with other valleys it lacks interest in the shape of impending crags and cliffs (although there is no more compelling skyline than that formed by the Buttermere and Grasmoor fells just around the corner to the south) but this deficiency is more than redeemed by its velvet pastures and neat woodlands, the latter occurring everywhere and giving the appearance of a park. Those now gone who settled here, to whom it was home and therefore the fairest place on earth, who first planned these sheltered farmsteads and valley communities, were great lovers of trees; and those who followed have, to their credit, taken good care of their heritage. Sweet Lorton!

(VI *Graystones 3*)

The Valley of Tarn Beck

Man rarely beautifies nature, but the exception most certainly occurs in the cultivated valleys of Lakeland. Every walker on the hills must often have been stopped in his tracks by some entrancing glimpse of beautiful green pastures and stately trees in a valley below, a perfect picture of charm and tranquillity in utter contrast to his own rugged surroundings. So delightfully fresh and sparkling, those lovely fields and meadows, that they seem to be in sunshine even in rain; so trim and well-kept that they might be the lawns of some great parkland. But they were not always so. Before man settled here these same valleys were dreary marshes.

The little valley of Tarn Beck illustrates the 'before and after' effect very well. Beyond and around the walled boundaries of the cultivated area – a patchwork of level pastures – there is at once a morass of bracken and coarse growth littered with stones, with much standing water that cannot escape the choke of vegetation. Once all the dale was like this. So was Borrowdale, and Langdale, and other valleys that today enchant the eye. Hard work and long perseverance have brought fertility from sterility. Rough hands have won a very rare beauty from the wilderness. . . . Man here has improved on nature.

(IV *Grey Friar 5*)

But precedence must be granted to Eskdale, the one valley that gives full allegiance to the Southern Fells and in some ways the most delectable of all. This is a valley where walkers really come into their own, a sanctuary of peace and solitude, a very special preserve for those who travel on foot.

(IV *Introduction*)

The Wythop Valley

The name is pronounced With-up locally. This quiet valley, almost unknown to Lakeland's visitors, is unique, not moulded at all to the usual pattern, a geographical freak.

The opening into it at Wythop Mill, between Sale Fell and Ling Fell, is so narrow and so embowered in trees that it might well pass without notice but for a signpost indicating a byway to Wythop Hall. Following this through a richly-wooded dell, the view up the valley opens suddenly beyond the farm of Eskin to reveal a lofty mountain directly ahead a few miles distant – a sight to stop explorers in their tracks. Of course all valleys run up into hills ... but what can this towering height be? ... Hearts quicken ... have we discovered an unknown 3000' peak? Wainwright's map on page 8 indicates no mountain ahead. ... Get out a *decent* map, the Ordnance Survey one-inch – and the truth slowly dawns ... why, of course ... it's dear old Skiddaw, of course, not immediately recognisable from this angle. ... But how odd! What an illusion! The valley certainly *appears* to lead directly to the mountain, *but*, completely out of sight and unsuspected from this viewpoint, the wide trench containing Bassenthwaite Lake profoundly interrupts the rising contours in the line of vision. The fact is that the Wythop valley, like all others, has hills along both sides, but instead of the normal steepening of ground at its head there occurs a sharp declivity to another (and major) valley system, the Derwent, occupied here by the unseen lake with Skiddaw rising from its far shore. The Wythop valley, elevated 600 feet above that of the Derwent, drains *away* from it, and the unobtrusive watershed (a meeting of green pastures and dark forest) may therefore be likened to a pass. The whole arrangement is unusual and remarkable.

Having described the valley as a freak, it is important to say also, and emphasise, that its scenery is in no way freakish. Here is a charming and secluded natural sanctuary in an idyllic setting, a place of calm, where a peaceful farming community husband the good earth now as for centuries past. Every rod, pole and perch of it is delightful and unspoilt. Motorcars can penetrate as far as Wythop Hall but happily are unaware of this. The valley is undisturbed and quiet; men still travel on horseback. There are five scattered farmsteads and, at the head, Wythop Hall, rich in story and legend. In days gone by the valley maintained a larger population and a church.

(VI *Sale Fell 3*)

17
VIEWS

Just to fill up this corner [of the diagram on the page], it might be mentioned that the two Lakeland Cats, -bells, and -stycam, appear directly in a straight line from this viewpoint only.
(VI *Causey Pike 7*)

Swirl How is a much better viewpoint for the man who would rather look at hills than at Millom, and moreover, the peace will not be shattered by squealing women and children and by knowledgeable males who noisily identify wrongly every hill in sight.
(IV *Coniston Old Man 17*)

The summit of Crinkle Crags is ageless, the cooling towers are symbols of one particular age. Here, on this rugged mountain-top, is an everlasting permanence, something *simple*, and we can understand; but *there* on the horizon, is something that is temporary, and complicated beyond our comprehension. Those modern structures, out of place in a landscape that is constant and unchanging, will vanish from the scene with the passing years. The mountains, nature's symbols of power and strength, will remain.
(IV *Crinkle Crags 19*)

By standing on tiptoes, craning the neck, leaping in the air and miscellaneous gyrations of the body not normally indulged in by people in their right senses, it is just possible, on a clear day, to see all the fells indicated on the diagram. The obstruction is caused by *Pinus mugo*, the gaunt bare branches of which form an unbroken screen up to ten feet high all round the cairn. This is unfortunate, because enough can be seen, with difficulty, to suggest that the view south, if uninter-rupted, would be simply glorious.

(v *Dodd 14*)

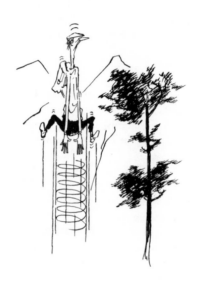

Lakeland is severed by a great geological fault; a deep trough running north and south across the district. Lakes of Winder-mere, Rydal Water, Grasmere and Thirlmere lie in this trough. The main road north of Ambleside takes advantage of that simple passage it affords, Dunmail Raise at 782′ being the highest point. The rift continues through the valley of St Johns and the Glenderaterra valley to Skiddaw Forest, where, situated exactly at its head, there rises the graceful cone of Great Calva. The trough is steeply bounded by high hills on both sides, notably the Helvellyn range. Great Calva's unique position provides it with a view along the direct line of the fault, so that, despite the mountains crowding into the scene, there is a remarkable vista, like looking along the sights a gun through the heart of the district to the low Windermere Fells in the extreme south.

(v *Great Calva 10*)

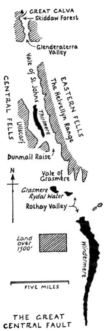

THE GREAT
CENTRAL FAULT

The only blot on the wide landscape is Calder Hall Atomic Power Station, a reminder that, down on the plains, men's thoughts are not, as they are up here, of mountains and peace and the bountiful goodness of the Creator of this lovely district. Here, not there, is the supreme artistry.

(iv *Great End 15*)

There is relief here for the conscientious chronicler of summit
views, the western half of the panorama being concealed by a
dense screen of fir and larch only a few yards from the cairn –
and he is surely not expected to climb the highest tree to see
what lies beyond.

The space thus saved by the lop-sided diagram is devoted,
as a special treat for readers, to a picture of the author
apparently contemplating the view (but more likely merely
wondering if it's time to be eating his sandwiches) from a
precarious stance on the edge of Raven Crag.

(III *Raven Crag 4*)

The bulky mass of Scafell Pike, north-east, obstructs the view
of a considerable slice of Lakeland, but nevertheless Scafell's
top is a most excellent viewpoint and, additionally, a place for
reverie, especially when reached from the north, for here
there is awareness that one has come at last to the outer edge

of the mountains and that, beyond, lie only declining foothills to the sea. Vaguely, in the mind of a fellwalker long past his youth, there arises a feeling of sadness, as though at this point the mountains are behind, in the past, and ahead is a commonplace world, a future in which mountains have no part, his own future. Yet this vision of low hills and green valleys, of distant sands and wide expanses of sea, is very beautiful. From Morecambe Bay to Furness and across the Duddon Estuary and Black Combe to the sand dunes of Ravenglass, and along the glorious length of Eskdale, all is smiling and serene, often when the high mountains are frowning. The bright pastures of Eskdale, won from the rough fells, have a happy quality of seeming to be in sunlight even under cloud. The view in this direction, unmarred by any scars of industry, is superb.

(IV *Scafell* 15)

There will never be general agreement on the answer to the question: which is the finest view in Lakeland?

Some views depend for their appeal on beauty of foreground, Tarn Hows for example; some on their intimate detail of a particular and pleasing feature, such as Castle Head's view of Derwentwater; some on colour and interesting arrangement, such as those from Ashness Bridge and Loughrigg Terrace. Other scenes have drama as their theme, Scafell Crag from Mickledore for example; popular, too, are the unforgettable birds-eye views from such heights as Great Gable and Great End, while many folk favour the most extensive prospects, as seen from Scafell Pike, Bowfell and Helvellyn. Opinions differ according to individual preference.

But for a classic view of the heart of Lakeland from a position on its perimeter Skiddaw Little Man must have majority support as the one place above all others. This viewpoint is detached and distant, and situated high above the wide vale of Keswick, so that the mountain skyline beyond is

seen across a great gulf, as if being approached by aeroplane, and sufficiently removed to admit correct perspectives and relationships. From this viewpoint, as the onlooker turns his gaze through the southern arc, the picture unfolds like the canvas of a master. This is Cinemascope *in excelsis*, on a scale never envisaged by Hollywood, a vast scene on a screen as wide as the heavens. And all of it is beautiful, nature's quiet artistry. Men are clever enough to make atomic bombs, and strut about like lords of creation, yet they can't even make a blade of grass or a sprig of heather, let alone build up a landscape like this. Which is as well.
(v *Skiddaw Little Man 13*)

Some walkers seem to experience a fierce joy in the sight of the Isle of Man in a view; others find greater pleasure in the sight of a first primrose in spring-time.

For the benefit of the former, the Isle of Man is shown in this diagram: it is visible from many Lakeland tops in good conditions, but from Swirl How its location can be determined particularly quickly for it appears exactly above the long flat top of Grey Friar nearby. The odds against seeing it at any given day are 50 to 1. At dusk or during night-bivouacs on the tops its position can be fixed in clear weather by the regular beams of its shore lighthouses. *But oh! the delights of that first primrose . . .*
(iv *Swirl How 10*)

Pride of place in the view must be given to Bassenthwaite Lake, directly below and seen in its entirety, intensely blue on a day of bright skies and then forming a beautiful picture enhanced often by the graceful sails of many yachts. All this can be viewed from a position of repose in fragrant and springy heather. On a warm day some resolution is needed to get back on one's feet and move on.
(v *Ullock Pike 8*)

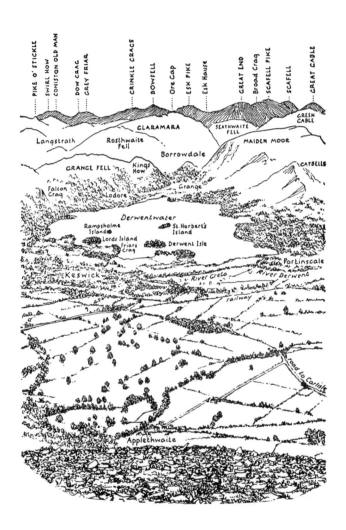

(v *Skiddaw Little Man* 4)

Walkers of a contrary turn of mind will summarily reject the advice to leave Armbroth Fell alone and may indeed be strengthened in their determination to climb it; nor are they likely to be deterred by the many TRESPASSERS WILL BE PROSECUTED notices that Manchester Corporation have sprinkled about the landscape. They would be further outraged if, having paid 12s 6d for this book, they found it did not cater for their idiosyncrasies by offering some details of routes of ascent.

(III *Armbroth Fell 2*)

None of the paths on the fell is continuous to the summit; a simple walk across grass from the main bridleway west of Iron Keld, however, soon brings it underfoot, and this is the easiest route to the top. Starts up the east flank may quickly lead to desperate manoeuvres in thick plantations.*

    * perhaps it should be made quite clear that this latter note is also intended for the guidance of walkers, not of courting couples.

(IV *Black Fell 3*)

The first lesson that every fellwalker learns, and learns afresh every time he goes on the hills, is that summits are almost invariably more distant, a good deal higher, and require greater effort, than expected. Fellwalking and wishful thinking have nothing in common.

    Here is an exception. This ascent may well be longer than expected, but the climbing is so very simple and the gradients so very easy, that the top cairn is reached, unbelievably,

before one has started to feel that enough has been done to earn it.
(VI *Dale Head* 7)

Honister Pass can only be reached on foot from Gatesgarthdale by walking along the motor road, but from Seatoller a good alternative is provided by the former toll road, which, being unfit for vehicles, has become a first-class walkers' way, in fact, a pedestrian by-pass. The surface is rough and rutted, but no fellwalker will object to this. It is the smooth hard surfaces of modern roads that tire the legs and feet, the monotony of repeating *ad nauseum* the same stride exactly. On rough ground no two movements are quite the same.

A good fellwalker never tramps a road that has a bus service.
(VI *Dale Head* 4)

The zig-zags above the tarn are tedious and often thronged with recumbent pedestrians.
(I *Dollywagon Pike* 5)

Easy buttress, *Easy* Gully and *Easy* Terrace are easy by rock-climbing, not walking, standards. Rock-climbers don't seem to know the meaning of easy. True, most walkers would manage to get up these places if a mad bull was in pursuit, but, if there is no such compelling circumstance, better they should reflect soberly . . . and turn away.
(IV *Dow Crag* 3)

*A shelter alongside the Walnc
Scar road, east of the pass,
just big enough for one persor
or a honeymoon couple*   (IV *Dow Crag 4*)

Following the old fence, all goes well, in spite of marsh patches, until the new forest fence is reached. With their customary disregard for walkers, the Forestry Commission have omitted to provide a stile. Get over, but mind your reproductive organs if wanted for future use.
(VII *Gavel Fell 8*)

The field-path is an excellent start on a day's walk on the hills; returning, when one no longer has strength left even to climb stiles and ambition has narrowed to the sole objective of reaching the bus terminus before collapse is complete, the road will be rather easier.
(IV *Glaramara 4*)

This is the true Lakeland of the fellwalker, the sort of terrain that calls him back time after time, the sort of memory that haunts his long winter exile.

It is not the pretty places – the flowery lanes of Grasmere or Derwentwater's wooded bays – that keep him restless in his bed; it is the magnificent ones.

Places like Great End . . .
(IV *Great End 2*)

Less time is required to do a round of the tops here – mile for mile – than, say, from Langdale or Wasdale with the further benefit that one can go back to bed for an hour following breakfast, or be 'home' in time for afternoon tea, or (which is to be preferred) spend extra time in quiet meditation amongst the lonely hills.
(v *Great Sca Fell 3*)

The hurdle across the gap in the wall at the top of the first enclosure is awkward to negotiate, being too frail to climb. Ladies, and gentlemen with short legs, will preserve dignity best by adopting the variation start marked A, so avoiding it.
(ii *Grey Crag 4*)

Solitary walkers who want a decent burial should bear in mind that if an accident befalls them in this wilderness their bones are likely to adorn the scene until they rot and disintegrate.
(ii *Grey Crag 6*)

A wire fence must be crossed (no stiles) – an easy task for long-legged walkers but others will be in some danger of bisecting themselves.
(vi *Grisedale Pike 9*)

A new fence must be crossed. It is not high, and can be stridden (or, if there is no such word, strided or strode – i.e. cock one leg over and then the other).
(VI *Hopegill Head 10*)

An advantage of solitary travel on the fells, greatly appreciated by all lone walkers, is the freedom to perform a certain function as and where one wishes, without any of the consultations and subterfuges necessitated by party travel. The narrow crest of the Knott Rigg ridge is no place for indulging the practice, however, whether alone or accompanied, walkers here being clearly outlined against the sky and in full view from two valleys. This comment is intended for males particularly. Women (according to an informant) have a different way of doing it.
(VI *Knott Rigg 3*)

Those walkers who, like the author, do not enjoy encounters with cows and young bulls and the sundry other mammals that commonly frequent confined farmyards will be relieved to learn that the routes illustrated have been specially selected to reduce this possibility to a minimum, and only at one place (Carhullan) is it necessary to pass through a farmyard.
(II *Loadpot Hill 8*)

Anybody who cannot manage this short and simple climb is advised to give up the idea of becoming a fellwalker.
(v *Longlands Fell 3*)

The step is not difficult to climb if the right foot is used first, the right foot in this case being the left. There is no dignity in the proceeding, either up or down.
(I *Low Pike 2*)

The walker who, preferring solitude, finds with dismay a procession of people engaged on the ascent may be recommended to tackle the climb by way of Birkside Gill where he may indulge his preference freely, for there he will not meet a soul (unless sheep have souls).
(I *Nethermost Pike 5*)

Once in a while every keen fellwalker should have a *prearranged* night out amongst the mountains. Time drags and the hours of darkness can be bitterly cold, but to be on the tops at dawn is a wonderful experience and much more than recompense for the temporary discomfort.

Hollow Stones is an excellent place for a bivouac, with a wide choice of overhanging boulders for shelter, many of which have been walled-up and made draught-proof by previous occupants. Watch the rising sun flush Scafell Crag and change a black silhouette into a rosy-pink castle! (This doesn't always happen. Sometimes it never stops raining.)
(IV *Scafell Pike 11*)

Variations of route may be adopted but time is a great enemy: the walk is lengthy (a feature most noticed when returning).
(IV *Scafell Pike 12*)

A certain amount of delectable clambering on rocky sections of the path is likely to prohibit its use generally by all and sundry (including the many Sunday afternoon picnic parties) which is a good thing for the genuine fellwalker.
(IV *Scafell Pike 15*)

Observant walkers will readily appreciate that it is not really necessary to climb the stile at the head of Far Easedale, the fence on both sides of it having vanished completely.
(III *Sergeant Man 7*)

Successful ascenders of the arete will be identifiable for some time thereafter by their blue lips and blue chins – bilberries thickly carpet the ground between 1500' and 2500 and fruit luxuriantly in season.

Inexperienced fellwalkers soon learn to distinguish, by trial and error, between bilberries and sheep-droppings, the former having decidedly the sweeter taste.
(V *Skiddaw Little Man 8*)

He who reaches Calf Crag with dry feet has cause to be satisfied with his boots.
(III *Steel Fell 9*)

The small crags around the summit offer practice for embryo climbers whose main concern is not too drop too far if they fall.
(I *Stone Arthur 4*)

Rock-climbers attracted to Brown Crag by the illustration on the previous page, expecting to see another Napes Needle, will turn away in disgust upon finding it only a few feet high. They may console themselves by trying to climb the nearby gorge in Brund Gill without getting wet.
(I *White Side 3*)

The use of the Bottom in Mountaineering
A fellwalker's best asset is a pair of strong legs; next best is a tough and rubbery bottom. In ascent this appendage is, of course, useless, but when descending steep grass or rocks such as are met with on the ridge of Yewbarrow the posterior is a valuable agent of friction, a sheet anchor with superb resistance to the pull of gravity.
(VII *Yewbarrow 7*)

19
WATER

The crowning glory of the Pikes, however, is the tarn from which they are named, cradled in a hollow just below the summit. Its indented shore and islets are features unusual in mountain tarns, and it has for long, and deservedly, been a special attraction for visitors to Patterdale. The charms of Angle Tarn, at all seasons of the year, are manifold: in scenic values it ranks amongst the best of Lakeland tarns.
(II *Angletarn Pikes 2*)

'The Bog' (with a capital T & B deservedly) is the official name of this morass. It may be said that here, at any rate, the foot of man has never trod (if it has, it must have made a horribly squelching sound!).
(III *Calf Crag 5*)

Dock Tarn is a place to lie adreaming, and life seems a sweet thing.
(III *Great Crag 3*)

This northern face is Harter Fell's chief glory, for here, too, a shelf cradles Small Water, which is the finest of Lakeland's tarns in the opinion of many qualified to judge: seen in storm, the picture is most impressive and awe-inspiring.
(II *Harter Fell 2*)

There is nothing pretty about Keppelcove Tarn and its sur-roundings. Here man tried to tame nature and in due course nature had its full revenge; between them they have made a mess of this corner of Lakeland.
(I *Helvellyn 16*)

Formerly these waters helped to irrigate the fertile Lowther and Eden valleys, but nowadays only the most favoured do so: the fate of the majority is captive travel along less pleasurable routes to the taps of Manchester, there to serve the needs of man in other ways.

(II *High Raise* 2)

TO BLEABERRY FELL – This is a walk to wish on one's worst enemy, especially after rain. There are many patches of swampy ground, necessitating wide detours.

TO HIGH TOVE – This is not a pleasant walk either. The hags of rich deep peat may be wonderful stuff for growing rhododendrons but seem singularly unattractive to walkers with soaking feet.

(III *High Seat* 7)

There is, of course, a natural affinity between mountains and lakes; they have developed side by side in the making of the earth. Often there is a special association between a particular mountain and a particular lake, so that, in calling the one to mind the other comes inevitably to mind also: they belong together. The best example of this is provided by Wastwater and the Screes, and perhaps next best is the combination of Mellbreak and Crummock Water, essential partners in a successful scenery enterprise, depending on each other for effectiveness. Crummock Water's eastern shore, below Grasmoor, is gay with life and colour – trees, pastures, farms, cattle, traffic, tents and people – but it is the view across the lake, where the water laps the sterile base of Mellbreak far beneath the mountain's dark escarpment, where loneliness, solitude and silence prevail; that makes the scene unforgettable.

(VII *Mellbreak* 2)

The tiny tarn at the foot of this crag has the unique habit of

There are good walkers and bad walkers, and the difference between them has nothing to do with performance in mileage or speed. The difference lies in the way they put their feet down.

A good walker is a *tidy* walker. He moves quietly, places his feet where his eyes tell him to, on beaten tracks treads firmly, avoids loose stones on steep ground, disturbs nothing. He is, by habit, an improver of paths.

A bad walker, is a *clumsy* walker. He moves noisily, disturbs the surface and even the foundations of paths by kicking up loose stones, tramples the verges until they disintegrate into debris. He is, by habit, a maker of bad tracks and a spoiler of good ones.

A good walker's special joy is zigzags, which he follows faithfully. A bad walker's special joy is in shortcutting and destroying zigzags.

All fellwalking accidents are the result of clumsiness.
(VII *Great Gable 16*)

Each entrance [to the fenced fell] is guarded by red danger signs. Prudent pedestrians will heed the warning and take no further interest in this page. What follows is therefore exclusively for the walker who (a) holds his life cheaply, or (b) reacts to such signs as a bull to a red rag. . . . Beware flying ammunition, of course.
(I *Great Mell Fell 3*)

Fellwalking is the healthiest and most satisfying of all outdoor exercises. Climbing the hills and tramping over the rough country makes a man strong and keeps him fit (it cleans his mind and does his soul good, too). But many enthusiasts, the author one of them, are nevertheless quite happy to reach the tops with a minimum of expenditure of effort, short of being carried upwards on the backs of their wives or other companions, which is simply not in the best traditions of fellwalking.

issuing *at both ends* after heavy rain. This shouldn't be possible!
(III *Silver How* 5)

The River Glenderamackin

The course of the Glenderamackin is remarkable. Starting as a
trickle from a marsh below the col linking Bannerdale Crags and
Blencathra, it soon gathers strength and aims purposefully for a
gap in the hills to the south, eager to be away from its desolate
place of birth and join other waters in a tranquil and pleasant
passage through Lakeland – for are not the streams of Lakeland
the most beautiful of all? But, alas, it cannot find a way across the
gap: a low barrier of land, Mousthwaite Col, defeats this object
and turns the young river east, and then – a greater disappointment – Souther Fell thrusts across the route. Now there is no
alternative but to go due north, and indications suggest that the
Eden Valley, and not Lakeland, is destined to receive its waters.
But, almost by a freak, it is prevented by a slight and otherwise
insignificant eminence at Mungrisdale from entering the Eden
catchment area and here it is again turned to the south. Hope
revives. Perhaps, after all, it may be permitted by friendly
contours at least to join some tributary of Ullswater? But no,
better still: after almost encircling Souther Fell a sudden glorious
view of Lakeland opens up to the west, the way thereto at last
being clear, and lying through sylvan meadows and rocky
gorges and woodlands and great lakes. Now the Glenderamackin
is no longer a neglected beck. It has become a river and men to
cross it must build bridges. It has acquired a stately loveliness, a
leisurely flow – it is a Lakeland river and therefore is beautiful.

An ambition has been realised, but it so nearly wasn't.
(v *Souther Fell* 3)

The new power-house at the foot of the lake, expelling the air
from its grills, is a useful drying-out place for wet walkers.
(IV *Whin Rigg* 5)

20

MISCELLANEA

In fell-climbing (as in other pursuits) there is a difference between *achievement* and *satisfaction*. One's sense of achievement is roughly in proportion to altitude gained by effort, but one's sense of satisfaction is not necessarily governed by the same rule. Lonely Ard Crags offers, especially in August, a climb up to a personal heaven of one's very own – at only 1800 feet
(VI *Ard Crags 3*)

The month of May is the best time for seeing the Dash valley. The hawthorn is a humble tree often straggly and untidy, but for a brief season in springtime it is transformed by a rare splendour.
(V *Bakestall 3*)

Hanging Stone – People with bad coughs should keep out of the line of fall.
(VII *Base Brown 4*)

The word 'carefully' is added to avoid ending the sentence with a preposition, which should never be used to end a sentence with.
(IV *Bowfell* 5)

Its slopes carry the Hayeswater aqueduct, and recent pipelaying operations there have left an ugly scar along its fair breast. Nature is a great healer: it cannot heal too swiftly here.
(II *Brock Crags* 1)

In this cairn is buried much broken glass, interred by the author after finding it scattered in the grass nearby. Broken glass is the worst sort of litter. Leaving it on ground where animals graze is *wickedness*.
(VI *Eel Crag* 7)

Here is a specimen timetable for the walk, travelling comfortably (slowly on the last lap)

Boot	10.00 am
Wha House	10.30
Cam Spout	12.30
Esk Hause	2.30
Esk Pike	3
Lingcove Bridge	4.30
Brotherilkeld	5.10
Wha House	5.30
Boot (direct)	6.15
Boot (via the bar of the Woolpack Inn)	?

(IV *Esk Pike* 7)

Much of Lakeland's appeal derives from the very lovely names of its mountains and valleys and lakes and rivers, which fit the scenery so well. These names were given by the earliest settlers, rough men, invaders and robbers: they were here long

before Wordsworth – but they, too, surely had poetry in their hearts?
(IV *Glaramara 2*)

note stretcher (just in case it is needed later in the day!)
(IV *Great End 6*)

To GREAT GABLE Follow everybody else.
(VII *Green Gable 8*)

TAKE CARE: DO NOT START FIRE and so waste the effort spent in drawing all the little trees on this map. The Forestry Commission, too, will be annoyed.
(IV *Harter Fell 4*)

Red Screes has more claims to distinction than any other high fell east of the Keswick–Windermere road——

(a) it has the biggest cairn;
(b) it has the greatest mileage of stone walls;
(c) it has one of the highest sheets of permanent standing water, and, in springtime, the highest resident population of tadpoles;
(d) it has the purest mountain form;
(e) it has the reddest screes and the greenest stone;
(f) it has one of the finest views (but not the most extensive nor the most beautiful) and *the* finest of the High Street range;
(g) it has the easiest way down;
(h) it offers alcoholic beverages at 1480';
(i) it gives birth to the stream with the most beautiful water-falls.

(Some of these statements are expressions of opinion; others, especially (h), are hard, facts.)
(I *Red Screes 12*)

Concave slopes are honest; convex slopes are deceitful. When ascending a concave slope the summit can be seen at all stages; on a convex slope it *seems* to be visible but what the climber sees is a skyline that recedes as he gains height. The final slope of Skiddaw above Randel Crag is an exasperating example of convexity.

(v *Skiddaw 16*)

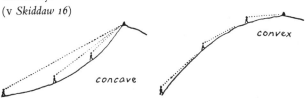

At this late stage in the book's preparation, space is becoming terribly short and cannot be spared for repetition of information already given. As the map of Scafell includes the whole area of Slight Side, would readers mind referring to pages Scafell 5–8?

(iv *Slight Side 2*)

(Telegraph poles removed from this view without permission of the P.O. Engineers)

(v *Souther Fell 1*)

from Mungrisdale,
obviously

The Beacon, Nab Crags
But for the stupid conduct of a party of schoolboys, there would have been an illustration here of a fine beacon that stood on Nab Crags for half a century: it was a conspicuous landmark, a reliable guide for shepherds on the fells in bad weather, and it kept alive locally a memory of the Wythburn man who built it.

The boys (on holiday a few years ago from a school outside the district) wilfully destroyed the beacon and rolled the stones down the fellside. *Two masters were with the party during this senseless act of vandalism; two brainless idiots, a disgrace to their profession. Lakeland can do without visitors of this type.*

Malicious damage is beyond pardon, and a source of endless trouble to farmers and shepherds. Rolling or throwing stones down the fellsides is CRIMINAL – sheep have been killed and crippled by such reprehensible folly.

Respectable walkers (readers of this book, for example) should *please* stop mischief of this sort whenever they witness it – and punish the offenders to the best of their ability.
(III *Ullscarf 9*)

row of ten cottages (ten chimneys, anyway)
(IV *Wetherlam 11*)

At the point marked ★ on the first branch road to the left (not used on this ascent) the author found (and pocketed) a cache of coins, to wit a threepenny-bit and two pennies. These will be restored to the loser upon receipt of a claim (the dates of the coins must be stated) attested by a responsible house-holder.
(VI *Whinlatter 4*)

21
SOME PERSONAL NOTES IN CONCLUSION

BOOK ONE: THE EASTERN FELLS

I suppose it might be said, to add impressiveness to the whole thing, that this book has been twenty years in the making, for it is so long, and more, since I first came from a smoky mill-town (forgive me Blackburn!) and beheld, from Orrest Head, a scene of great loveliness, a fascinating paradise, Lakeland's mountains and trees and water. That was the first time I had looked upon beauty, or imagined it, even. Afterwards I went often, whenever I could, and always my eyes were lifted to the hills. I was to find then, and it has been so ever since, a spiritual and physical satisfaction in climbing mountains – and a tranquil mind upon reaching their summits, as though I had escaped from the disappointments and unkindnesses of life and emerged above them into a new world, a better world.

But this is by the way. In those early Lakeland days I served my apprenticeship faithfully, learning all the time. At first, the hills were frightening, moody giants, and I a timid Gulliver, but very gradually through the years we became acquaintances and much later firm friends.

In due course I came to live within sight of the hills, and I was well content. If I could not be climbing, I was happy to sit idly and dream of them, serenely. Then came a restlessness and the feeling that it was not enough to take their gifts and do nothing in return. I must dedicate something of myself, the best part of me, to them. I started to write about them, and to draw pictures of them. Doing these things, I found they were still giving and I still receiving, for a great pleasure filled me when I was so engaged – I had found a new way of escape to them and from all else less worth while.

Thus it comes about that I have written this book. Not for material gain, welcome though that would be (you see I have not escaped entirely!); not for the benefit of my contemporaries, though if it brings them also to the hills I shall be well pleased; certainly not for posterity, about which I can work up no enthusiasm at all. No, this book has been written, carefully and with infinite patience, for my own pleasure and because it has seemed to bring the hills to my own fireside. If it has merit, it is because the hills have merit.

I started the book determined that everything in it should be perfect, with the consequence that I spent the first six months filling wastepaper baskets. Only then did I accept what I should have known and acknowledged from the start – that nothing created by man is perfect, or can hope to be; and having thus consoled and cheered my hurt conceit I got along like a house on fire. So let me be the first to say it: this book is full of imperfections. But let me dare also to say that (apart from many minor blemishes of which I am already deeply conscious and have no wish to be reminded) it is free from inaccuracies.

The group of fells I have named the Eastern Fells are old favourites, not quite as exciting as the Scafell heights, perhaps, but enjoyable territory for the walker. They are most conveniently climbed from the west, which is a pity, for the finest approaches are from the Patterdale valley to the east. The walking is easy for the most part; very easy along the main watershed. The coves below the summits eastwards are a feature of these hills: rarely visited, they are very impressive in their craggy surroundings. Exploration also reveals many interesting evidences of old and abandoned industries – quarries, mines, aqueducts, disused paths. Somebody should write a geographical history of these enterprises before all records are lost.

Some of my experiences during many solitary wanderings while collecting information for this book would be worth the telling, but I preserve the memories for the time when I can no longer climb. One, however, returns insistently to mind ... I remember a sunny day in the wilderness of Ruthwaite Cove: I lay idly on the warm rocks alongside Hard Tarn, with desolation everywhere but in my heart, where was peace. The air was still; there was no sound, and nothing in view but the shattered confusion of rocks all around. I might have been the last man in a dead world. A tiny splash drew my gaze to the crystal-clear depths of the tarn ... a newt was swimming there, just beneath the surface. I watched it for a long time. And I fell to wondering ... wondering about it, and its mission as it circled the smooth waters, and the purpose of its life – and mine. A trivial thing to remember, maybe, yet I do. I often think of that small creature, a speck of life in the immensity of desolation in which it had its being.

It is a remarkable thing, now that I come to think of it, that I still set forth for a day on the hills with the eagerness I felt when they were new to me. So it is that I have thoroughly enjoyed my walks whilst this book has been in preparation, much more so because I have walked with a purpose. Yet recently my gaze has been wandering more and more from the path, and away to the fells east of Kirkstone – my next area of exploration.

So, although I take my leave of the Eastern Fells with very real regret, as one parts from good friends, I look forward to equally happy days on the Far Eastern Fells. When this last sentence is written Book One will be finished, and in the same moment Book Two will take its place in my thoughts.

Christmas, 1954

BOOK TWO: THE FAR EASTERN FELLS

It would be very remiss of me if I did not take this first
opportunity publicly to acknowledge, with sincere gratitude,
the many kind and encouraging letters that followed the
publication of Book One. There have also been offers of
hospitality, of transport (I have no car nor any wish for one),
of company and collaboration, and of financial help – all of
which I have declined as gracefully as I could whilst feeling
deeply appreciative, for I am stubbornly resolved that this
must be a single-handed effort. I have set myself this task, and
I am pigheaded enough to want to do it without help. So far,
everything is all right. Sufficient copies of Book One were
sold to pay the printer's bill, and here again I must thank all
readers who recommended the book to others, for it is per-
fectly clear that, lacking full facilities for publicity and distri-
bution, it could hardly have succeeded otherwise.

I have just completed the last page of Book Two, and feel
like a man who has come home from a long and lonely
journey. Rarely did I meet anyone on my exploration of the
High Street fells. Usually I walked from morning till dusk
without a sight of human beings. This is the way I like it, but
what joys have been mine that other folk should share! Let
me make a plea for the exhilarating hills that form the subject
of this book. They should not remain neglected. To walk upon
them, to tramp the ridges, to look from their tops across miles
of glorious country, is constant delight. But the miles are
long, and from one place of accommodation to another they
are many. The Far Eastern Fells are for the strong walker and
should please the solitary man of keen observation and imagination. Animal and bird life is much in evidence and not the
least of the especial charms of the area is the frequent sight of
herds of ponies and deer that make these wild heights their
home.

Perhaps I have been a little unkind to Manchester Corporation in referring to Mardale and Swindale in this book. If we can accept as absolutely necessary the conversion of Haweswater, then it must be conceded that Manchester have done the job as unobtrusively as possible. Mardale is still a noble valley. But man works with such clumsy hands! Gone for ever are the quiet wooded bays and shingly shores that Nature had fashioned so sweetly in the Haweswater of old; how aggressively ugly is the tidemark of the new Haweswater! A cardinal mistake has been made, from the walker's point of view, in choosing the site for the new hotel: much more convenient would have been a re-built Dun Bull at the head of the valley, or better still amongst the trees of The Rigg. For a walker who can call upon transport, however, the new road gives splendid access to the heart of the fells.

I leave this area to renew acquaintance with the more popular and frequented heights in the middle of Lakeland – the Langdale, Grasmere and Keswick triangle. This is a beautiful part of the district, and I shall enjoy it; but it is a weakness of mine to be for ever looking back, and often I shall reflect on the haunting loneliness of High Street and the supreme loveliness of Ullswater. It will please me then to think that this book may perhaps help to introduce to others the quiet delights that have been mine during the past two years.

Autumn, 1956

BOOK THREE: THE CENTRAL FELLS

If I were thirty years younger I should already be looking forward to the time when, with the seventh and last book in this series finished (round about 1965) I could start to go over all the ground once again with a view to making such revisions as may be found to be necessary. I fear, however, that by that time age will have shackled my limbs to such an extent that the joyful task may be beyond me.

Guidebooks that are inaccurate and unreliable are worse than none at all, and I am aware that in a few small respects

Books One and Two are already out of date. It is most exasperating, for instance, to learn of fences appearing on land where I have shown none, or of the erection of new buildings, or that signposts or cairns have been destroyed or established – all in the short interval since the books were originally published. Even as I write, there is a proposal afoot to demolish the dam at Stickle Tarn, which would shrink considerably the size of the tarn, and alter its shape – and this news comes to me only a few days after sending to the printer several pages which feature the tarn and on which its present proportions are most carefully delineated. There is no stopping these changes – but I do wish people would leave things alone! Substantially, of course, the books will be useful for many years to come, especially in the detail and description of the fell tops, while the views will remain unaltered for ever, assuming that falling satellites and other fancy gadgets of man's invention don't blow God's far worthier creations to bits. But, this dire possibility apart, the books must inevitably show more and more inaccuracies as the years go by. Therefore, because it is unlikely that there will ever be revised editions, and because I should just hate to see my name on anything that could not be relied on, the probability is that the books will progressively be withdrawn from publication after a currency of a few years.

All this is leading to a suggestion that readers who are really enthusiastic about fellwalking and have several more seasons of happy wandering to look forward to, should start to use these volumes as basic notebooks for their own personal records, making such amendments (neatly, I hope!) as they find necessary during their walks and adapting the page-margins for dates and details of their own ascents and other notes of special interest.

I had intended (under pressure from publisher, printer and booksellers alike) to demonstrate in these final pages that an

increase in the price of the books had become urgently necessary to cover rising costs of production – but I haven't left
myself enough space to do it; besides, I have no stomach for
such unpalatable discourse. So for the time being the price
will continue uniform at 12s 6d – let's say for the sake of
tidiness.

Away with such trivial matters! It is better by far that my
last few lines should tell of the Central Fells, even though this
area will already be well known to most readers and in places
is much frequented; indeed the presence of other walkers was
often rather an embarrassment to me, although my mission
was never suspected. The popular heights above Derwentwater
I left until the holiday crowds (and Vivian Fisher, *and* his
gate!) had all departed from the scene. Alone, what a celestial
beauty I found there in the quiet of late autumn and early
winter! What rich warm colours! I walked on golden carpets
between golden tapestries, marvelling anew at the supreme
craftsmanship that had created so great a loveliness, and at my
own good fortune to be in its midst, enjoying a heaven I had
done nothing to deserve. One cannot find the words to
describe it: only an inexpressible humility fills the heart . . .

12s 6d, 15s, 17s 6d – what does it matter?

I must hasten now to the Scafells, noblest of Lakeland's
cathedrals, while good health and appreciation of beauty and
simple reverence and gratitude remain with me, for when I
have lost these blessings I shall have little left. This one lesson,
above all others, the hills have taught me.

New Year, 1958

BOOK FOUR: THE SOUTHERN FELLS
I have said my farewells to Mickledore and Esk Hause and
Bowfell and all the other grand places described in this book,
with the same 'hollow' feeling one has when taking leave of
friends knowing that it may be for the last time. For the next

few years I shall be engaged elsewhere, to the north and west, and although I shall be straining my eyes to see these old favourites from afar, I shall not be visiting them during this period; and perhaps never again.

There has been a clamour for Book Four ever since the first in the series appeared, and there is no doubt at all that the region of the Southern Fells has priority in the minds of most lovers of the Lake District, and especially those whose joy it is to walk upon the mountains. I agree, without saying a word to detract from the merits of other areas. All Lakeland is exquisitely beautiful; the Southern Fells just happen to be a bit of heaven fallen upon the earth.

The past two years, spent preparing the book, have been a grand experience – in spite of countless ascents of Rossett Gill (which, incidentally, seems to get easier if you keep on doing it). Fortune smiled on me hugely during the months I had set aside for the Scafells – day after day of magnificent weather, with visibility so amazingly good that one simply got used to seeing the Scottish hills and the Isle of Man permanently on the horizon. I had feared delays on the Scafells by unsuitable conditions or even normal weather, but this never happened. Many glorious mountain days, followed by happy evenings in Wasdale and Eskdale – that was the pattern for the summer of 1959.

It has taken me over 300 pages to describe the fells in this area, and I need say no more about them; but I must emphasise the supreme beauty of the approaches along the valleys – every yard of the way to the tops, and every minute of every day, is utter joy. But a special word for Eskdale: this is walkers' territory par excellence, and as traffic in other valleys increases, it is likely to become the last stronghold for travellers on foot. This lovely valley is quiet and unfrequented. I rarely met anybody when climbing out of Eskdale but, on reaching the watershed, found the ridges alive with folk who had come up from Borrowdale and Langdale.

Great Langdale is a growing problem. This used to be a walkers' valley too, and one of the best. Nowadays walkers are beginning to feel out of place. Coaches, cars, caravans, motor-bikes, and tents throng the valley. One cannot complain about people who want to see the scenery but some of the characters infesting the place at weekends have eyes only for mischief. These slovenly layabouts, of both sexes, cause endless damage and trouble, and it behoves all respectable visitors (still in the majority) to help the police and farmers to preserve order. Poor Langdale! How green was my valley!

I finished the Langdale tops in 1958 but had occasion to return in the spring of 1959. Glancing up from the valley to the cairn on Pike o'Blisco (as I always do) I was dismayed to notice that it had been mutilated. I went up to see and found that the tall column of stones had been beheaded, the top part having been demolished, apparently by human agency. Are the wreckers getting up on the tops too? . . . If all readers who visit this summit will replace one stone firmly, please, the cairn may in time again look as it does in the Pike o'Blisco chapter.

I ought to mention that I am aware that the Duddon Valley is also properly known as Dunnerdale, a name I haven't used in the book, preferring the former; just as I never refer to Blencathra by its better known modern name of Saddleback. It's a matter of personal choice. I like the Duddon Valley and Blencathra. I don't like Dunnerdale and Saddleback.

Several letters, and even petitions, from Great Gable enthusiasts have been sent in asking me to do Book Seven next after Book Four, and Book Five last. What a frightfully untidy suggestion! It springs from a generally accepted view, of course, that there is nothing 'back o' Skidda' worth exploring. I want to go and find out. There is a big tract of lonely fells here, wild and desolate; but this is immortal ground, the John Peel country, and I rely further on a centuries-old saying that

'Caldbeck Fells are worth all England else'. A land rich with promise, surely!

On this occasion I intend to make an excuse for defects in penmanship. I am going to lay the blame fairly and squarely on the head of Cindy, a Sealyham puppy with roving eyes, introduced to the household some time ago. Cindy has shown absolutely no sympathy whatever with my efforts to write a classic – a fearful waste of time when I might otherwise be tickling her tummy or throwing her ball or having a tug-of-war with an old stocking. The persistent pokings and tuggings at critical moments of concentration must have resulted in inferior work, for which I am sorry. But it's Cindy's fault, not mine.

Christmas 1959

BOOK FIVE: THE NORTHERN FELLS

Well, that's another finished.

Up to two years ago I hadn't known the Northern Fells intimately, and the remoter parts I had known merely as names on the map. Imaginative and romantic names, many of them: Arm o'Grain, Red Covercloth, Frozen Fell, Ward Steel, Balliway Rigg, Thief Gills, Trusmadoor, Whitewater

Dash, Brandy Gill, Black Nettle Hause, Candleseaves Bog, and others. Significantly, these names, foreign-sounding in Lakeland, are all of wild places in the hills, and it would seem that many of them can be attributed to the mining prospectors who first explored these uplands some five or six centuries ago, giving identity to the various landmarks. Down in the surrounding valleys, though, the dalesfolk adopted traditional Lakeland names for their farms and local features – 'thwaite', 'dale' and 'beck' occurring everywhere.

The era of mining activity has largely passed, barytes being the only mineral now being won, and the hills are quiet again. The creatures of the high places are undisturbed. Even in summer, few walkers visit the tops. In winter the Blencathra pack roam the fellsides occasionally. Both summer and winter, Pearson Dalton crosses the hills with his dogs, twice a week making the journey between his home at Fell Side and the lonely Skiddaw House, where he is shepherd. The only sounds are the call of the birds, the cries of sheep, the murmur of streams, and wind rustling the coarse bents and heather. There are no false notes in this peaceful symphony, no discords, no harshness. This is a land of solitude and silence.

On the southern fringe of the group Skiddaw and Blencathra are, however, old favourites. Skiddaw is climbed by the popular path from Keswick every day of the year, often by scores and sometimes by hundreds of people. And Blencathra is deservedly a much-visited peak. These two apart, the only other fell on which I saw another person in the whole of my walks, and then at a distance, was Carrock Fell, and this happened on three different occasions. As for the rest – nobody, not a soul, not once. I felt I was preparing a book that would have no readers at all, a script that would have no players and no public. Nevertheless, these were glorious days for me – days of absolute freedom, days of feeling like the only man on earth. No crowds to dodge, no noisy chatter, no litter. Just me, and the sheep, and singing larks overhead. All of us well content.

I must not eulogise the Northern Fells too much. These lonely hills do not compare at all for grand scenery and situations with those of Wasdale and Langdale and Borrowdale. (But Blencathra and Carrock Fell and the Ullock Pike ridge of Skiddaw are very definite exceptions that would rank high in any company.) Generally, they are not in the same class. From a walkers point of view, Caldbeck Fells are NOT 'worth all England else'. But they have one great attraction the others are fast losing – for the walker who prefers solitude, for the naturalist, they offer undisturbed enjoyment at all seasons of the year. They are a perfect Bank Holiday refuge. They are just right, too, for the aged hiker who can no longer force his jaded legs up Rossett Gill or around Mickledore – here, on gentler gradients, is a new lease of life for him.

Skiddaw Forest, magnificent walking country very reminiscent of Scotland, is under a threat. Engineers have their eyes on this vast gathering ground, and possibly an impounding reservoir will occupy the floor of this basin, or the Caldew valley, before long. If it does, this book will badly need revision. Why can't these high and mighty public bodies be content with *surplus* water only (goodness knows, there's plenty!), piping it to reservoirs built in their own areas?

I must mention the grand people of the little communities around the base of these fells, especially in the remote north. Holiday-makers have made very little impact here. Sturdily independent, here are folk, unspoiled by 'tourism', whose roots go deep in their own soil. Ever alert for sights and sounds on the fellside or in the valley fields, their work is their life. It is a pleasure to be in their company, an honour to be in their confidence. John Peel was not the only worthy character raised in these parts.

All my walks during the past few years have ended at

Keswick Bus Station, where there is a splendid open view of the mountains between Borrowdale and Bassenthwaite, a tremendously exciting array of sharp peaks and lofty ridges. Sometimes, in winter, I have seen them as a black silhouette, or silvered by moonlight, against the fading colours of the western sky; and, in summer, purpling in the dusk of evening with a skyline edged in gold. These are the North-Western Fells, which I have long considered the most delectable of all. Envy me my next two years, for this is the area next on my programme. Ready, Easter 1964, old Kruschev willing.

I thank those readers who helped to restore the cairn on Pike o'Blisco. A correspondent now tells me that the fine column on Lingmell has been wantonly thrown down. I hardly like to mention it, but ... do you mind? Next time you're passing?

Autumn, 1961

BOOK SIX: THE NORTH WESTERN FELLS
When concluding Book Five I expressed the opinion that the North Western Fells were the most delectable of all, and, after two years in their charming company, I hold to that view. In other areas I have sometimes tired a little of repeatedly tramping the same tracks, but not here. Times without number I came off the hills faced with a long trudge down Whinlatter, or along the Coledale mine road or Newlands, until every stone and every tree became familiar, but never, rain or shine, did I do so wearily, but only regretting that another day was done, that another week must pass before I could return. Always I was lingering, always looking back.

All this territory is wonderful walking country. Much of it, south of the Grisedale Pike ridge, is well known and needs no introduction (although I have just completed nearly 300 pages doing that!). Even so, there are many corners rarely visited, many excellent routes rarely trodden, many interesting features rarely seen. Several of the lines of ascent described in this book are as good as anything else in Lakeland, which is saying a lot, yet the majority of walkers are unaware of them. Searchers after traces of ancient history or old industrial activity will find much of interest. Geologists and botanists are well catered for here. Photographers cannot fail to produce beautiful pictures.

On the whole, the walking is quite excellent. The hills are easier to climb than their abrupt appearance suggests: the secret is to get on the ridges early, because it is the ridges, not the fellsides, that provide the best travelling underfoot and the finest views, and give the area its special appeal.

Newlands is a privileged valley, not only extraordinarily pleasant in itself but ringed by grand fells; for a quiet fellwalking holiday there is no better centre. Borrowdale we all know and love, but this valley is not so well placed for the area, and is nowadays so busy with cars that its joys are best experienced in winter. Buttermere is beautiful, but a better base for the Western Fells than the North Western. I ought to put in a good word for Thornthwaite Forest, to the north of Whinlatter, which, in spite of much afforestation, is a fascinating place to explore. I never saw a soul here in eight months' weekend wandering, except once when I found myself mixed up in a foxhunt. Nothing in this region pleased me more than the shy Wythop Valley, so easy to walk, so charming and unspoiled, a little tranquil world apart.

Several times I came down to Buttermere, and it was hard to deny myself an occasional excursion to the magnificent mountains on the far side, but now the time has come when I am free to do this, and Book Seven will tell of High Stile and of Great Gable and Pillar and others that yet remain unrecorded. If I say that I start upon the last book in the series with mixed feelings, many of you will know what I mean.

Autumn, 1963

BOOK SEVEN: THE WESTERN FELLS

When I came down from Starling Dodd on the 10th of September 1965 I had just succeeded in obtaining a complete view from the summit before the mist descended, after laying patient siege to it through several wet weekends, and in so doing I had concluded the field-work for my last book with only one week left before the end of the summer bus service put the fell out of reach. Thus a 13-year plan was finished one week ahead of schedule. Happy? Yes, I was happy, as anyone must be who comes to the end of a long road ahead of the clock. Sorry? Yes, I was sorry, as anyone must be who comes to the end of a long road he has enjoyed travelling. Relieved? Yes, I was relieved, because a broken leg during these years would have meant a broken heart, too.

I think I must concede that the scenery of the western half of Lakeland (dropping a vertical through High Raise in the Central Fells) is, on the whole, better than the eastern, although it has nothing more beautiful than the head of Ullswater. This is not to say that the fellwalking is better: it is more exciting and exacting but the Helvellyn and High Street ranges in the east are supreme for the man who likes to stride out over the tops all day. Those who prefer to follow narrow ridges from summit to summit are best catered for in the west. The southern half, too, is generally finer than the northern, so that the highlights of the district are to be found mainly in the south western sector, from the Duddon to Whinlatter. But it is all delectable country . . . One advantage I found in roaming around the Western Fells is that they are still free from the type of visitor who has spoiled Langdale and Keswick and other places easier of access. Wasdale Head and Buttermere are beginning to suffer from tourist invasion, but on the tops one can still wander in solitude and enjoy the freedom characteristic of the whole district before somebody invented the motor car.

I promised to give my opinion of the six best fells. I should not have used the word 'best', which suggests that some are not as good as others. I think they are all good. The finest, however, must have the attributes of mountains, i.e., height, a commanding appearance, a good view, steepness and ruggedness: qualities that are most pronounced in the volcanic area of the south-western sector. I now give, after much biting of finger-nails, what I consider to be the finest half-dozen:

SCAFELL PIKE
BOWFELL
PILLAR
GREAT GABLE
BLENCATHRA
CRINKLE CRAGS

These are not necessarily the six fells I like best. It grieves me to have to omit Haystacks (most of all), Langdale Pikes, Place Fell, Carrock Fell and some others simply because they do not measure up in altitude to the grander mountains. There will be surprise at the omission of Scafell, the crags of which provide the finest sight in Lakeland, but too much of this fell is lacking in interest. It would be seventh if there were seven in the list. Contrary to general opinion (which would favour Great Gable), the grandest of the lot is Scafell Pike. Of the six, all are of volcanic rock with the exception of Blencathra.

The six best summits (attributes: a small neat peak of naked rock with a good view) I consider to be

DOW CRAG, Coniston
HARTER FELL, Eskdale
HELM CRAG, Grasmere
EAGLE CRAG, Langstrath
SLIGHT SIDE, Scafell
STEEPLE, Ennerdale

All these, except Steeple, are accessible only by scrambling on rock. The top inches of Helm Crag are hardest to reach.

The six best places for a fellwalker to be (other than summits) because of their exciting situations, and which can be reached without danger, are

> STRIDING EDGE, Helvellyn
> First col, LORD'S RAKE, Scafell
> MICKLEDORE, Scafell
> SHARP EDGE, Blencathra
> SOUTH TRAVERSE, Great Gable
> SHAMROCK TRAVERSE, Pillar

Of course I haven't forgotten Jack's Rake on Pavey Ark. I never could. But this is a place only for men with hair on their chests. I am sorry to omit Great Slab and Climbers Traverse on Bowfell.

The finest ridge-walks are, I think,

> THE FAIRFIELD HORSESHOE (Ambleside)
> THE HIGH STREET RANGE (Garburn – Moor Divock)
> THE MOSEDALE HORSESHOE (Wasdale Head)
> CAUSEY PIKE – WHITELESS PIKE
> GRISEDALE PIKE – WHITESIDE
> ESK HAUSE – WRYNOSE PASS, via Bowfell
> THE ESKDALE HORSESHOE (Slight Side – Bowfell)
> THE HELVELLYN RANGE (Grisedale Pass – Threlkeld)
> THE HIGH STILE RANGE, with Haystacks
> CATBELLS – DALE HEAD – HINDSCARTH – SCOPE END
> THE CONISTON ROUND (Old Man – Wetherlam)
> (not in order of merit)

In my introductory remarks to Book One I described my task in compiling these books as a labour of love. So it has been. These have been the best years for me, the golden years. I have had a full reward in a thousand happy days on the fells.

But, unexpectedly, it has been a profitable venture for me in terms of money, bringing me a small fortune, simply through the continued support of the many kind readers who have both bought and recommended the books. It is money I have not spent and do not want. One surely does not wish to be paid in cash for writing a love-letter! There is, or soon will be, enough to build and equip an Animal Welfare Centre in Kendal, and the Westmorland Branch of the R.S.P.C.A. have accepted for this purpose a gift which is really donated by the readers of these books. Every true fellwalker develops a liking and compassion for birds and animals, the solitary walker especially for they are his only companions, and it seems to be appropriate that this windfall should be used to provide a refuge in Lakeland where ailing and distressed creatures can be brought for care and attention. I thought you would like to know this. You have provided the bricks.

If Starling Dodd had been the last walk of all for me, and this the last book, I should now be desolate indeed, like a lover who has lost his loved one, and the future would have the bleakness of death. I have long known this and anticipated it, and sought desperately in my mind for some new avenue along which I could continue to express my devotion to Lakeland within the talents available to me. I am in better case than the lover who has lost his loved one, for my beloved is still there and faithful, and if there were to be a separation the defection would be mine. But why need this be the last book? Within a year I shall be retired from work (on account of old age!), but I can still walk, still draw, still write; and love itself is never pensioned off . . . So there must be other books . . . In this series I have crowded details of the fells into some 2000 pages, but as much as I have included has been omitted through lack of space. I would like now, in a more leisurely fashion, to continue acquaintance with the fells, and, out of consideration for my white hair, explore the valleys and daleheads more. What I have in mind is A LAKELAND SKETCHBOOK, which, all being well, could be the start of a new series that would aim to show the best of Lakeland in pictures and, by indicating the changes taking place in the district, in valley and on fell, serve to supplement the present series of guidebooks. I also have a good title for another book: FELL WANDERER, and might do this first if I can think of something to write about – personal experiences on the fells perhaps – not, definitely not, an autobiography (as if I dare! Let me keep my friends!). In between times I am pledged to do A PICTORIAL GUIDE TO THE PENNINE WAY, and have had four collaborators, four good men and true, sweating their guts out during the past year to provide a mass of detail and resolve certain doubts and generally smooth my own journey subsequently. This will be a unique book the way I plan it: you will start it at the bottom of the last page and you will read upwards and forwards to the top of the first, which is something that even the Chinese never thought of doing. It will seem logical, however, when you see it, and there is no question of your having to stand on your head.

Regretfully, I reject suggestions of a Book Eight: 'The Outlying Fells'. . . . So this is farewell to the present series of books.

The fleeting hour of life of those who love the hills is quickly spent, but the hills are eternal. Always there will be the lonely ridge, the dancing beck, the silent forest; always there will be the exhilaration of the summits. These are for the seeking, and those who seek and find while there is yet time will be blessed both in mind and body.

I wish you all many happy days on the fells in the years ahead.

There will be fair winds and foul, days of sun and days of rain. But enjoy them all.

Good walking! And don't forget – watch where you are putting your feet.

Christmas, 1965

'The day before had been sullen and wet and so was the day following, but that morning was perfect. The sun rose steadily in a blue sky. I left him as he had requested, beside Innominate Tarn, and the larks sang a song of welcome.'

INDEX

Note: Fells in SMALL CAPITALS are those which have a chapter of their own in the Pictorial Guides; folios in *italic* refer to specific landscape features shown in the diagrams and drawings.